Living & praying
the
LORD'S PRAYER

Published by
The Bible Reading Fellowship
First Floor, Elsfield Hall
15–17 Elsfield Way, Oxford OX2 8FG
ISBN 1 84101 182 7

First published 2002
10 9 8 7 6 5 4 3 2 1 0

Acknowledgments
Unless otherwise stated, scripture quotations are taken from The New
Revised Standard Version of the Bible, Anglicized Edition, copyright
© 1989, 1995 by the Division of Christian Education of the National
Council of the Churches of Christ in the USA, and are used by
permission. All rights reserved.

Scripture quotations taken from the Holy Bible, New International
Version, copyright © 1973, 1978, 1984 by International Bible
Society, are used by permission of Hodder & Stoughton Limited. All
rights reserved. 'NIV' is a registered trademark of International Bible
Society. UK trademark number 1448790.

A catalogue record for this book is available from the British Library

Printed and bound in Great Britain by
Omnia Books Limited, Glasgow

Living & praying
the
LORD'S PRAYER

Peter Graves

For
Matthew, Luke and Ellie
In love and gratitude

CONTENTS

SPIRITUALITY IN AN AGE OF CHANGE

Although bored by organized religion, many today are fascinated by the figure of Jesus. Frustrated by the superficiality of our age, they are hungry for something that will satisfy the deeply spiritual longings within. This should not surprise us. A few years ago a Gallup Poll asked Americans with which historical figure they would most like to spend a day. Some 65 per cent chose Jesus, 37 per cent of whom claimed no church allegiance. In Britain too there are many who, although deeply inspired by the life and work of Jesus and hungry for spiritual depth, still remain outside the Church.

In the spring of 2000, the National Gallery in London staged an art exhibition entitled 'Seeing Salvation'. It explored ways in which the person of Jesus and the significance of his life and ministry have been portrayed through 2000 years of history. Specially prepared to celebrate the Millennium, it soon became the best-attended exhibition ever held in the gallery. Thousands not only flocked to it but also viewed the art with great seriousness, reverence and awe. An accompanying series of TV programmes was watched by millions.

On a visit to the States in 1992, I bought a copy of a fascinating and in many ways prophetic book, which introduced me to the work of the 'futurologist'. *Megatrends 2000*, by John Naisbitt and Patricia Aburdene (William Morrow & Co., 1990), outlined some of the enormous changes that would be taking place as the Millennium dawned. Numerous such books have continued to warn us that change will increasingly touch every area of our lives and by now even the most superficial observer knows that this is happening. Indeed the rapidity of such change is difficult to keep up with. It is accelerating so fast that new computers, for example, are almost out of date before they are marketed.

Of particular interest is the assertion of Naisbitt and Aburdene that the need for spiritual belief is intensified in times of great change. They prophesied a 'revival of religion', and this is already being seen in the worldwide growth of Christianity and Islam, and the increasing activity of fundamentalist groups in both religions. In the West, contemporary interest in Eastern religions is becoming more and more obvious. The popularity of yoga, meditation, holistic medicine and the human potential movement all point to a renewed interest in the spiritual. There is nothing particularly remarkable about this, since it is faith that helps us make sense of our experience and find the resources needed to cope with the ever-changing landscape of our lives.

Since the Enlightenment of the 18th century, we have almost worshipped science, technology and the idea of progress, as if they were themselves a religion. Now, however, it is becoming increasingly obvious that science will not solve all our problems. Indeed we recognize that our sophisticated technology can just as easily create 'hell' as 'heaven'. More and more nations have access to nuclear weapons and some of them are ruled by regimes that are far from stable. Global warming, climate changes and the depletion of the ozone layer all remind us of the urgency of ecological concerns. The techniques of genetic engineering are becoming ever more advanced, and many people are concerned that such skills could be used irresponsibly with disastrous consequences. With fear in their hearts, many wonder just what the future holds. Accordingly they turn to religion to discover meaning, purpose and a framework for responsible living. Although they may be fascinated by the person and teaching of Jesus and are perhaps actively looking for peace and a sense of well-being, sadly not many of them are finding it in the Church. The spirit of our age may be summed up in the words, 'Spirituality, yes! Organized religion, no!'

All this presents the Church with an enormous opportunity and challenge. Perhaps in our presentation of the gospel we have been over-cerebral for too long. People need to get in touch once again with the soul. Perhaps without knowing it, they are looking for a living experience of God that touches their innermost being. Through meditation and prayer, not necessarily in a Christian context, they seek to discover and deepen such experience. Many in the Church are also looking for new depth in their spirituality, and long to rediscover a sense of the closeness of God and the power of prayer.

Against such a background, this book seeks to explore the spirituality of Jesus and to do so through exploring the prayer that Jesus taught us, the prayer we know as the Lord's Prayer. Through it we learn how to pray and we also discover the essence of the teaching of Jesus. It is my prayer that as you use the prayer and reflect on its meaning, your experience of God will be deepened and enriched, and the life of faith will become more real and vital.

THE ORIGINS OF THIS BOOK

A few years ago, when I was minister of Cullercoats Methodist Church, near Newcastle upon Tyne, we decided to organize a series of house-groups for Bible study, discussion and prayer. The idea was not warmly received. People said they would prefer an expert to teach them, and were worried about taking part in discussion groups because they did not feel they knew enough. Indeed a number were concerned that such groups would lead to the 'pooling of ignorance' rather than the sharing of faith. After considerable discussion we decided to go ahead with a pilot project. We would study the Lord's Prayer together, because, as they said, 'We know it so well, we don't think about the words.'

Leaders were trained, study material prepared, and midweek groups held. On the preceding Sunday evenings a series of sermons was preached, giving basic teaching on the Lord's Prayer. Some members of each group made a special point of attending these services so that they could share what they had learned with others at the weekly meeting. The series really was a great success, and the congregation insisted that such house-groups should become a regular feature of church life. The fellowship and teaching had been so special that people wanted more. When asked why they felt there had been such a change of attitude towards the whole idea of house-meetings, they all replied that it was the choice of subject. They felt that they knew the Lord's Prayer, and this gave them confidence to share their knowledge and experience and ask their questions. It took them deeper into the experience of prayer, enriched their understanding of Christian doctrine and enabled them to get to know other members of the church better. Thus they experienced the power and richness of true fellowship.

This study also helped me, the minister. In preparing the sermons and study materials, I realized that I had long taken the Lord's Prayer for granted, and been much too shallow in my understanding of it. Over the years since then, I have gone on exploring it, and have shared my findings both in the local church and beyond. A series of broadcasts on Premier Radio in London led to a most encouraging response. The Bible studies I led at the Methodist 'Easter People' convention in 1999 convinced me of the real need for teaching on this subject. A sabbatical has since given me the opportunity to reflect further, read more widely and eventually write this book. I do so in the hope that it might give enough background to help ordinary Christians grow in their faith and enable both individuals and groups to discover the teaching of Jesus in more depth. It is for all who want to explore the prayer more fully and thereby make it more truly their own.

At the end of each chapter I have provided suggestions for Bible study and discussion, to help both individuals and groups to reflect on the studies in this book. Devotional materials and suggestions for prayer and meditation are also provided to help us deepen our experience of praying the Lord's Prayer instead of just studying the words of a masterpiece.

Because each study group is different, I have provided more material than is needed for just one meeting. This will enable the leaders to select the approach likely to be the most helpful for their own particular group. There is, of course, no virtue in getting through all the questions for their own sake. Rather, we should use those questions that particularly further our own discovery of the relevance and power of the words of Jesus.

Cell groups meeting in homes, churches, colleges and places of work do provide a wonderful opportunity for people to grow and discover together the riches of their faith. For some, though, this will be a new experience. I have therefore included a brief appendix to give some basic guidelines to help and encourage those wishing to organize such groups.

The Lord's Prayer, in its traditional form, is very widely known, used and loved by many who never attend church but are still interested in spiritual matters. I realize, of course, that many churches now use a more contemporary form of it, but I have chosen to use the better-known version, believing it to be most accessible to the majority of people.

I am deeply grateful to all who have helped in the production of this book, not least to my wife Tricia and our children, Matt, Luke and Ellie, who have supported me in so many ways. The guidance, encouragement and patience of Naomi Starkey, my editor at BRF, is greatly appreciated. She has shared her wisdom and experience in most helpful ways. Dr Brian Beck of Cambridge, Dr Donald Haynes of Asheboro North Carolina, Professor Wilfred Weber PhD MD and Dr Malcolm White, both of Westminster Central Hall, have all offered much encouragement. Their many helpful suggestions and comments are greatly appreciated.

I hope I have acknowledged all the quotations used, but if not, I apologize. My understanding has been enriched by so many fellow travellers over the years that I may well have quoted them without realizing it. In such cases, I have made their words my own because they have touched me so deeply, and I hope that, realizing such to be the case, they will deem it a compliment and forgive me.

Chapter 1

THE LORD'S PRAYER IN CONTEXT

I have never found prayer easy. Indeed, as a young Christian in my teens, I could never understand how prayer could make any difference either to me or to our needy world. What was the point of just talking to God and hoping something would happen? No matter how much we prayed, needs and problems still surrounded us, so why bother? Surely Christianity was all about doing the will of God rather than just thinking about it.

While I was wrestling with such questions, a very wise minister confessed that he was one of the world's least mechanical and technical people. He did not know how the engine of a car worked, but he still drove one and enjoyed doing so. In fact, he wondered how he had ever managed to get anything done before he owned a car. Likewise, he suggested, we should not let our lack of understanding prevent us from exploring the life of prayer. We should keep on praying, and in so doing would discover riches beyond our imagining.

The questions still remained, but I took his advice, and over the years have come to appreciate prayer more and more. I have also come to realize that I used to view prayer as primarily a matter of asking God's help or seeking his strength. I now know that this is just one small part it. Prayer involves an ongoing relationship with God that touches every aspect of life.

My reference to car engines reminds me of a poster sometimes seen on church notice boards. It proclaims, 'God's your engine, not your spare tyre!' All too often we turn to God when troubles burden us or crises come our way. We use prayer as if it were little more than 'first aid' for an emergency, when really, in both good and bad times, it should be a resource to strengthen and sustain us, no matter what happens.

Such a 'spare tyre' approach is only scraping the surface of prayer. God longs to be the driving force in our lives, but he will not force himself upon us. Respecting our freedom, he patiently waits until we are ready and willing to follow him, and then he leads us forward. Through prayer we seek to be in tune with his will and be empowered to do it. From this it will be seen that prayer and life are intimately linked together.

LIVING AND PRAYING

A visit to Lindisfarne is an inspiring experience. Normally called Holy Island, it is situated just off the Northumberland coast and in clear view of the ancient home of the kings of Northumbria, Bamburgh Castle. Here, inspired by saints like Cuthbert and Aidan, the Celtic monks spent time in their communities of prayer. The island was chosen specially because at high tide each day it is cut off, but at low tide one can cross over the narrow causeway to the mainland beyond. The tide safeguarded the balance of their life, keeping them on the island for prayer but then sending them back to the mainland to live out their prayers as they engaged in mission and service.

On a recent visit to the great industrial city of Coventry, I spent some time in the Chapel of Christ the Servant. Because its focus is upon the work of the Church in industry, it is in a way symbolic of the life of the city itself. The chapel is circular in shape. This is particularly appropriate since, in so many religions, the circle is a symbol of wholeness. Although an integral part of the cathedral, it juts out from the main wall of the sanctuary, thus giving the impression that Christ and his Church are being thrust into the world where they must be the servant of all. Their ministry is to lead people in their search for wholeness. Thus we see the integration of prayer and work, and a harmony between spirituality and life, the sacred and the secular. To reflect on the design of this chapel is to be reminded that Christianity is not about entering some religious ivory tower, cut off from everyday life. It is rather a challenge to make God's work our own, and also a call to pray for and serve the world he loves. We enter a church for worship, prayer, fellowship and celebration, but we leave it so as to be involved in mission, service and daily living. This is all part of the gospel of wholeness. Prayer and work go together.

This interrelationship between prayer and life is so important. Without it, says Michael Ramsey, prayer becomes no more than a 'pious, cultural or aesthetic pursuit'. When prayer is clearly linked with the needs of the real world, however, it stops the Christian life from becoming 'a kind of aggressive busyness, which misses the humility and inner peace which communion with God can bring'.[1]

True prayer and worship, therefore, are not a withdrawal from the world and its problems. Rather, they bring the needs of the world into God's presence and seek new insight and strength to enable us to play our part in making the world a better place.

In full and hectic lives, it is all too easy for God to be squeezed out to the sidelines. We need to make space so that we can be truly open to him. Many great Christians, like John Wesley, taught that the busier we are likely to be, the more time we need to spend in prayer. They felt it most important to keep their lives in focus and so needed to be in close communion with God. In modern business parlance we would say, 'It's not a matter of working harder, but smarter.'

This is emphasized by the example of Jesus himself, who spent much time in prayer, especially at the crisis points of his ministry. This never stopped him working for the furtherance of the kingdom, however. It kept him in touch with his Father, and was the driving force of his life and ministry. In short, if we are too busy to pray, we are too busy!

This healthy balance between spirituality and life is certainly seen in the Lord's Prayer. Very much a prayer centred on God's nature and purpose, it still seeks help for quite specific human needs. Inspired by a vision of the perfect will of God being done 'on earth as it is in heaven', it sees the kingdom of God invading earth and being lived out here.

Perhaps I can best sum up the point of this section in the words of Ignatius Loyola: 'Pray as if everything depended upon God, and work as if everything depended on you!'

PRAYER AS A RELATIONSHIP WITH GOD

Before the word 'Christian' was used, disciples were known as 'followers of the Way'. Christian discipleship is all about 'abiding in Christ' and following the Master who ever leads us forward. It involves our having a relationship with God, from which appropriate behaviour and action must come.

By their very nature, relationships cannot stand still. Either they grow and deepen or they wither and die. God wants our relationship with him to be an ever-growing experience, an adventure and a voyage of discovery. In short, we are pilgrims journeying towards a goal. This is why prayer is so important. Essentially it is the means whereby our relationship with God can be deepened and enriched. It involves the sharing of our whole selves with God and discovering who he is.

Christianity has often been described as a 'transforming friendship'. Although it sounds too good to be true, Jesus our Lord and Master is also our friend and brother. He pays us the enormous compliment of wanting us to enter and sustain a living relationship with him. Of course, this must be reflected in the quality of our living and our faithful obedience to his teaching, but it is deepened and strengthened through the life of prayer.

As in any friendship, our relationship with God is sometimes very relaxing. We find ourselves enjoying a sense of his presence. I once heard Father Michael Hollings, the well-known Catholic writer and broadcaster, speak of the value and importance of 'wasting time with God'. After all, just being together is part of what relationships are all about.

At other times, prayer is hard work. It can be very frustrating, especially when we don't feel we are really getting through to God. Nevertheless, it is worth all the effort, for through it we learn more about ourselves, the meaning of our lives, and God.

Self-discovery is thus another important aspect of prayer. Concerned about the superficiality of so much contemporary life, many are becoming increasingly aware of the importance of the 'inner journey'. At times we need to turn away from the haste of our daily lives, so as to be still and relax in the presence of God. Only then can we let our souls catch up with our bodies. We must have time to reflect, to examine our thoughts and actions and to get our priorities sorted out.

Sometimes we need to be released from the 'tyranny of the urgent' so as to dwell on the really important. As the Americans say, 'the main thing is to keep the main thing as the main thing!' It is all too easy to be sidetracked into the trivial, or to become so wrapped up with the immediate that we lose sight of the ultimate. To avoid such distractions, we need to focus more on God and his purpose for our lives. Then, with his help and the guidance we so desperately need, we are enabled to live in a deeper, more reflective and purposeful way.

This reflection on the deeper aspects of our lives is aided by the fact that we can be completely real with God. Since he knows us better than we know ourselves, it is pointless trying to hide anything from him or pretend that we are what we are not. We don't need to wear a mask. Instead we know it's safe to share our joy, thanksgiving, sorrow and pain with him. The more we reveal our innermost being to him, the richer is our experience of his love, acceptance, forgiveness and renewal.

Prayer also deepens our concern for others and our relationship with them. Our intercession is an act of love. Through it we hold the anguish of the world in the healing and compassionate heart of God.

Michael Ramsey says that intercession is 'to bear others on the heart in God's presence'. We pray in the name of Jesus, which means that 'we learn to bend our wantings to our glimpses of the divine will'. Intercession is not a matter of our bombarding God with our requests, but rather 'the bringing of our desires within the stream of God's own compassion'. He points out that the 'compassion of God flows ceaselessly towards the world, but seems to wait upon the co-operation of human wills in obedience and prayer'.[2]

Similarly, Father Harry Williams points out that prayer involves an 'identification with those for whom we pray, reflecting on their circumstances and lifting them into his presence, and holding them there for a short while'. It is like putting ourselves at their disposal before God, sharing their hurt and its transformation into richness and glory. We 'share their Good Fridays so we can see them irradiated with Easter glory'.[3]

Because prayer touches the whole of life, it is often born of pain, grows through praise, requires persistence and leads to a deep sense of inner peace and harmony. We can see something of this in the Lord's Prayer.

Sometimes our deepest prayer arises from pain and heartache. When everything seems to go wrong and the bottom drops out of our world, we cry out in desperation to God. We may feel a deep sense of injustice, anger and frustration, and justifiably pray, 'Deliver us from evil.' We want him to transform sorrow into joy and bring hope from despair. Feeling something of the anguish of the cross, we long for resurrection.

It has been well said that 'praise is the darkroom that changes our negatives into positives'. To focus on the goodness of God helps put our problems into perspective. Sometimes we marvel at the beauty of creation, the goodness of life, the reality of answered prayer and the sheer abundance of God's blessings. Prayer then flows from a sense of praise and thanksgiving, and we find ourselves glorifying God as we pray, 'Hallowed be thy name; thy kingdom come on earth as it is in heaven.'

Although we naturally share our longings with God, we want them to be in tune with his perfect will, and so with persistence we pray, 'Thy kingdom come, thy will be done, on earth as it is in heaven.'

When we come to God in pain, our prayers often begin with us wrestling with God. As we experience his healing power, we begin to discover the deep sense of inner peace and harmony that comes from surrender to his perfect will. Knowing we are in his hands, we receive inner assurance that all will be well. We are in the everlasting arms of 'our Father who art in heaven', and he will never let us fall.

THE ANSWERS TO PRAYER MAY SURPRISE US

Of course, we do not automatically receive what we ask for. After all, prayer is not a magical means whereby we can manipulate God and force him to do our will. Neither is God some kind of celestial messenger boy, waiting to run to do our bidding just because we press a bell. Prayer is much more a matter of our seeking to be open to God and his work in our lives.

A small child may create a fuss because her parents refuse to do what she wants. Because of their experience the parents realize how wrong or even dangerous it would be to accede to her request. Similarly, our view of reality is often limited and biased, so it is a good thing that we do not always receive the answer we hope for. God sees things from a bigger perspective. Because he is aware of every dimension, he sometimes needs to say 'No', 'Not yet', or 'Let me show you another way'.

Experience shows that God sometimes answers prayer by changing the circumstances that trouble us, but alternatively he supplies sufficient power to overcome them. Often it takes time for us to discern how God is answering our prayer, so we need to pray with persistence. As Augustine of Hippo reminds us, God does not ask us to tell him our needs so that he can learn about them, but so as to make us 'capable of receiving his gifts'.

BE ENCOURAGED: THE PRAYER IS BRIEF!

Just out of college, but not yet ordained, I served as a Probationer Minister in a small church in Hertfordshire. We invited a group of Anglican nuns to come and share in a special evening service during which we could reflect together on the life of prayer. They shared many profound and helpful insights with us. Then came the final question: 'From all your years in the religious life, what is the main thing you have learned about prayer?' The reply was unanimous and it surprised us all. They said, 'Keep it simple!'

If those who have given their lives to prayer can give such advice, then maybe there's hope for us all. Many feel inadequate or even guilty when the subject of prayer is raised. They have heard of saints and great Christian leaders spending hours in prayer and meditation, whereas they find it difficult to spend even a few minutes quietly focusing on God and bringing their concerns to him. In a burst of enthusiasm or a surge of discipline, some decide to commit half an hour or more to prayer and Bible reading each day. After a few minutes, though, they have run out of ideas, don't know how to use the time, and so give up in despair. They say, 'It's all too complicated for me. I'll leave it to the vicar. He's trained to do that sort of thing.'

The Lord's Prayer is deceptively simple and remarkably brief. The NRSV translation gives Luke's version in just 38 words and that of Matthew in 58. So be encouraged! The important thing is that you pray, not that you spend hours doing so. It is better to decide to spend five or six minutes a day in prayer, and then find that you need more time, than to set yourself an unrealistic target. To do so could lead to giving up and then feeling a failure. Prayer can be brief, to the point, and extremely effective. Start small, and let your experience of praying grow naturally. But, be warned, the more you grow in the life of prayer, the more time you will find yourself wanting to pray!

The brevity of the Lord's Prayer does not detract from its relevance and power. It can be recited in almost any circumstances. Not only is it a form of words to be used, it is also a framework around which we can build our own prayers. It enables us to catch a glimpse of the prayer life of Jesus himself, and gives rich insight into his teaching. It certainly relates well to the real world, not least to the pain, praise, persistence and peace which, as we have seen, are important aspects of the life of prayer.

The African theologian Tertullian (c.160–230) wrote the earliest known commentary on the Lord's Prayer. He says that it embraces 'as it were the whole of the Lord's discourses, the whole record of his instruction: so that without exaggeration there is comprised in the prayer an epitome of the entire gospel'.[4]

This may be something of an exaggeration, but it certainly alludes to the Prayer's succinctness and reminds us that much of the teaching of Jesus does point us back to the phrases of the Lord's Prayer.

In subsequent chapters we shall work through the Lord's Prayer clause by clause and seek to explore its depths, but before we do so, it is important to see it in context.

THE BIBLICAL CONTEXT

The Lord's Prayer is found in the Gospels of Luke and Matthew, but the form and context in each is very different. Luke's version of the Prayer is slightly shorter than that of Matthew. It addresses God simply as 'Father', and so reflects the mode of address Jesus would normally have used when speaking to God. It also stresses the intimacy that was the hallmark of the prayer life of our Lord, and from which the disciples were learning so much.

Much of the Gospel of Matthew is related to the needs of the early Church, as it sought to apply the teaching of Jesus to its own context and to contemporary Christian experience. It is not surprising, therefore, to find Matthew using the more familiar opening words, 'Our Father'. In using this form of address, the prayers of each individual were linked with those of the whole community of faith. His version is almost identical to the form we use today. It includes all the phrases we use that are not found in Luke, namely, 'who art in heaven'; 'thy will be done on earth as it is in heaven'; and 'but deliver us from evil'. Such words are typical of the liturgical phrases used in the Jewish prayer and worship of the time. Since most of his readers were Jewish Christians, these phrases would sound familiar and so reassure them in the practice of prayer. They would also encourage readers in the development of their faith. The version of Luke, on the other hand, may well reflect the usage of Gentile Christian communities.

We cannot be absolutely sure of the exact circumstances in which Jesus gave this prayer to his disciples. He probably shared it with them on several different occasions and may have done so in a slightly different form. Most scholars, however, tend to think that perhaps Luke's shorter version was the original and that Matthew has enlarged it with a little Jewish paraphrase.

The context in Luke

Even though he had a closer relationship with God than any other human, Jesus still needed time with the Father. In the Gospels we frequently find him going away to a lonely place to pray. This is especially so in Luke's Gospel, for Luke constantly emphasizes the place of prayer in the life of the Master. Indeed, before any major event in his life, Jesus spent much time in prayer. Luke wants to emphasize that, for both Jesus and his followers, crucial decisions should be made in full dependence upon God and in obedience to his will.

Like all Jewish children, the disciples would have been instructed in daily prayer and synagogue worship from childhood. Those of us who find prayer difficult can take comfort from the fact that even with such a background, the disciples still sought help. Having watched Jesus at prayer, they were attracted by the very special intimacy that he had with the Father. Doubtless it was because of this that they came with the request, 'Lord, teach us to pray, as John taught his disciples' (Luke 11:1).

In response Jesus followed the approach of the rabbis and probably of John the Baptist as well. The Jews understood prayer as something that was taught and learnt by each generation and then handed on to the next. This sense of tradition gave it credibility and grounded it in the experience of God's dealings with his people throughout history. Rather than giving a lecture, Jesus told them that when they prayed they should say the Lord's Prayer. He gave them a form of words to be used as a kind of 'identity badge', which would remind them of their commitment to the way of Jesus. It should not surprise us that it was thoroughly Jewish in style. After all, much of what Jesus taught about prayer, he would have learnt himself from the scriptures and his Jewish heritage.

The prayer itself is found in Luke 11:3–4. It is immediately followed by the parable of the friend at midnight:

And he said to them, 'Suppose one of you has a friend and you go to him at midnight and say to him, "Friend, lend me three loaves of bread; for a friend of mine has arrived, and I have nothing to set before him." And he answers from within, "Do not bother me; the door has already been locked, and my children are with me in bed; I cannot get up and give you anything." I tell you, even though he will not get up and give him anything because he is his friend, at least because of his persistence he will get up and give him whatever he needs.'
LUKE 11:5–8

Here the stress is on persistence, not because God is unwilling to answer our prayers, but rather because he is encouraging us to take prayer seriously and realize its value.

Travellers in the Middle East depended upon hospitality for their accommodation. To avoid the midday heat, many would journey in the evening and might therefore arrive late and unannounced. A solemn obligation was placed upon the host by the laws of hospitality: he must provide for them. Such an obligation would have justified the host in waking his neighbour, even though this would have meant disturbing the whole household. The family would have slept close together on mats on the floor, and nobody could have got up without the risk of waking the others. The point to note in this parable is the contrast between the ways of God and the behaviour of people. Through the shameless persistence of his friend, a sleepy and unwilling householder can in the end be coerced to give him what he needs. If we humans behave in such a way, then how much more will God, our loving Father, supply all the needs of his children.

This does not, of course, absolve us from intensity in our praying. Indeed the very passion of our prayers can show something of their sincerity and the depth of our longing. The important thing is that we are not wringing gifts from an unwilling God, and even when he says 'No' the answer still comes from his love and wisdom.

This is emphasized by the fact that the parable is followed by a challenge: 'Ask, and it will be given to you; search, and you will find; knock, and the door will be opened for you' (Luke 11:9). To ask, to search and to knock are all ways of deepening our relationship with

God. They are also very active words. There is nothing shallow or superficial in them, and they say nothing about being vaguely interested. Audacious as it may seem, we are encouraged to come to God with persistence, faith and determination.

The early Church knew the living presence of God to be with them in every situation. No doubt this is reflected in the statement, 'If you then, who are evil, know how to give good gifts to your children, how much more will the heavenly Father give the Holy Spirit to those who ask him!' (Luke 11:13).

Matthew speaks of the Father giving 'good things' to those who ask him. Luke's reference to the Holy Spirit could be a modification of the original. Not only is it not found in Matthew 7:1–11, the equivalent passage in Matthew, but it seems to intrude unexpectedly into the context, and is not taken up in what follows. Brian Beck suggests that this is to avoid a materialistic interpretation of 'good things'. Luke wishes to avoid any reference to the possibility of material gain from trusting in God.[5] Our calling is to store up treasures in heaven (Luke 12:21).

Frances Hogan stresses the spiritual significance of this reference to the Holy Spirit. She suggests that instead of just giving us gifts, God gives the Holy Spirit 'who is the source of all the gifts and graces we need to further the kingdom. Jesus wants His disciples to have the same anointing with power that He had himself'.[6]

Out of the generosity of his heart, God offers us so much more than we could ever dream possible, but he does not want us to take his generosity for granted. Luke therefore encourages us to pray in faith and trust, and to do so with persistence.

The context in Matthew

In Matthew 6, the context is different. The Lord's Prayer is recorded as part of the Sermon on the Mount, itself a summary of the teaching of Jesus. As we have seen already, Matthew is writing for Jewish Christians, so his version has a much more obviously Jewish feel to it.

Oscar Cullman points out that the first three petitions are reminiscent of the Jewish Kaddish prayer, albeit in a rather different form.

There are also parallels with the 'eighteen benedictions', Jewish prayers that, although they did not reach their final form until AD70–100, were used in synagogue worship at the time of Jesus.[7] Brian Dodd adds that 'the Lord's Prayer was used in the early church in exactly the same way as were the "eighteen benedictions" in the synagogues of the day'. He says, 'Both were used as an outline for prayer; the wording in both was flexible; both followed the same form, praise–petition–praise; both were used for congregational and private prayer; both were customarily prayed three times a day.'[8]

Jewish prayers of the time were not firmly fixed, but were spoken freely with additions and omissions. Thus the idea that the Lord's Prayer should be used both as a prayer in its own right and as a pattern into which we can fit our own prayers and concerns is quite in accord with contemporary Jewish practice.

In this section of the Sermon on the Mount, Jesus deals with the three traditional forms of Jewish piety—alms, prayer and fasting. The stress is on single-minded devotion. The three sections of Matthew 6:1–18 all make the same point: almsgiving, prayer and fasting are to be done for God alone, in secret, and not for human praise. Those who do them for human adulation have their reward already. Because their motives are wrong, they will miss out on the blessings God longs to share with his children.

Jesus powerfully contrasts the showiness of the Pharisees and other hypocrites with the humble Christian alone in his room. The hypocrites wanted everyone to see them so that they would be regarded as 'super-spiritual'. The Christian, on the other hand, does not seek human praise. He comes in response to the call of God, and does so in sincerity and without any pretence.

Likewise, the humble prayer of Christian disciples is very different from the mindless babbling of pagans. For them, prayer was a sort of magic, which they hoped would enable them to get what they wanted. It was a kind of artillery barrage directed at the Almighty. Presumably they felt that unless they kept pushing, their gods might fall down on the job. Thus they kept praying so that all opposition to their desires would be overcome. Matthew stresses the importance of humility.

When we are consumed by pride, we become so full of ourselves that God cannot get a look in. It is only the humble who are open to receive from God.

We have now explored the context of the Lord's Prayer, so we are ready to look at its content in more detail. In the next chapter, we shall explore how it might help us in our own search for an ever-deepening relationship with 'Our Father'.

FOR USE IN SMALL GROUPS

GROUP BIBLE STUDY

Read Luke 11:1–13 and Matthew 6:1–18.
- Note the differences between each version.
- Divide the group into two, and ask one half to look at the context in Matthew and the other in Luke. What teaching on prayer do we find in our passage? How does it relate specifically to the Lord's Prayer?
- Bring the whole group together to share what they have learned and discuss it. What are the key things Jesus teaches us about prayer?

Read 1 Kings 18:20–39.
As you reflect on the story of Elijah and the prophets of Baal on Mount Carmel, contrast the pagan approach to prayer with that of Elijah. What are the major differences? Compare this with the teaching of Jesus in Matthew 6:7–13.

FOR DISCUSSION

1 The Lord's Prayer has been described as a 'pattern prayer' and as a 'simple framework which enables us to express things in our own way'. How important is it for you to have a pattern for prayer? What frameworks have you found most helpful in your own praying?

2 'You have been born anew, not of perishable but of imperishable seed, through the living and enduring word of God' (1 Peter 1:23). The seed of the gospel has been planted within us. It is the source of a new way of life, which should bear the fruits of love. All seeds have to be nourished if they are to grow. How and why should we seek such nourishment in Bible study and in prayer? What is the relationship between the two? In what other ways is our faith nourished?

FOR PRAYER AND REFLECTION

A prayer exercise

Ask each member of the group to choose a prayer that has been particularly meaningful to them, to write it out and bring it to the next meeting. Next time you meet, ask them to read their chosen prayer and say why they have found it so special. Each member can then exchange their prayer with another so as to use them in their own devotions. Some members might like to build up a scrapbook of prayers that are special to them, or perhaps one member might like to compile one for the group as a whole.

A prayer to use

Eternal God, the light of the minds that know thee, the joy of the hearts that love thee, the strength of the wills that serve thee; grant us so to know thee that we may truly love thee, so to love thee that we may fully serve thee, whose service is perfect freedom.

GELASIAN SACRAMENTARY

(AN ANCIENT BOOK OF TEXTS AND PRAYERS FOR THE CELEBRATION OF THE EUCHARIST)

Chapter 2

'THE END OF ALL OUR EXPLORING'

As we pray the Lord's Prayer, we start by calling God 'Our Father', but the more we grow in our relationship with him, the more we realize that we have only just begun. We have a lot more learning to do before we really understand what it means to know him personally as our loving Father. After all, there is a great difference between knowing something in the mind and realizing it in the heart. In his quartet 'Little Gidding', T.S. Eliot writes:

> *We shall not cease from exploration*
> *And the end of all our exploring*
> *Will be to arrive where we started*
> *And know the place for the first time.*

Perhaps this is best illustrated by looking at the well-known parable of the prodigal son (Luke 15:11–32). Although we shall look at this in more detail in our next chapter, it is worth pointing out now that, as the story begins, both brothers would have thought they really knew their father. Presumably they had lived with him all their lives. However, their approach to him was dominated by legalism instead of love. They had the mistaken idea that all he was interested in was their service and obedience. In a way, they had become slaves to duty, whereas the father longed to treat them as sons. The younger son found this restrictive. As far as he was concerned, there was a whole world waiting for him beyond the confines of his father's village. He wanted the freedom to explore it, but finished up in a state of degradation. He had become a slave to debauchery and eventually to poverty and hunger. It was only when he returned home, back where he started, that he began to realize the depths of his father's love. It was as if he had come to know him for the first time.

FROM BONDAGE TO FREEDOM

The biblical idea of salvation is often expressed in terms of release from slavery and the discovery of true freedom. This is seen supremely in the death and resurrection of Jesus. Through his sacrificial love he offers freedom from the captivity of sin and so releases us to realize our fullest potential. We do this by becoming his followers. Captivated by his love and a vision of what life should be, we find a commitment that gives a framework for living. A great sense of security comes from knowing that we are the children of God. We discover that life does have purpose and meaning. We are given the freedom to live on a big map and explore the life of discipleship.

The same image is emphasized throughout the pages of the Old Testament. The first occurrence of the idea of God as father comes when Moses marches in boldly to stand before Pharaoh and proclaims, 'Thus says the Lord: Israel is my firstborn son. I said to you, "Let my son go that he may worship me"' (Exodus 4:22–23). So, to call God 'father' was strongly linked with the hope of freedom.

Thus the story of the Exodus begins. It is in itself the key to understanding the history of Israel. Scholars speak of 'salvation history', and observe that God intervened in human affairs to enable his chosen people to escape from the bondage of slavery in Egypt to the freedom of the Promised Land. On the way, they had many wilderness experiences, made many discoveries and had a lot of learning to do, but they had found freedom and they were moving forward.

In the previous chapter we saw that prayer is an ever-deepening relationship with God. We turn now to two key questions. How can we find such a relationship? And how can the Lord's Prayer help us make such a relationship our own?

A very wise and experienced professor was instructing his students on the art of preaching. Your job, he said, is 'to make the familiar strange'. He went on to explain that most people in church on Sunday morning think they know the Bible and the teachings of the faith. Many have been 'sermon-hardened' over the years, and come with no sense of expectancy. They hear only what they want to hear. The students were called to 'open a few windows', to provide new insights into old truths and so enable their congregations to see things in a new light.

Many of us learned the Lord's Prayer in childhood, and most of us know it so well that we take it for granted. We may use it in almost every act of public worship and can sometimes find ourselves saying the words without thinking. We too need to see it in a new light.

THROUGH THE WILDERNESS

I gained fresh insight into the Lord's Prayer through the writing of Anthony Bloom, the Russian Orthodox archbishop who is more formally known as Metropolitan Anthony of Sourozh. In his book *Living Prayer*, he emphasizes that the Lord's Prayer is not only a prayer but also 'a whole way of life expressed in the form of a prayer'.[1] He says that if we start at the end we can see how it paints a picture of the gradual ascent of a soul from bondage to freedom. He then leads us on a fascinating journey beginning with the petition 'Deliver us from evil'. Through it all, he skilfully relates the Lord's Prayer both to the Old Testament story and to our contemporary spiritual search. Just as the Israelites made their exodus journey from slavery in Egypt to the freedom of the Promised Land, so we move from the bondage of selfishness and sin to the freedom of sonship whereby we can call God 'Father'. First, though, the Israelites had to pass through the wilderness, and so do we.

The wilderness has deep significance in scripture. It is not just a geographical location. It is a place of formation for the people of God, the place where we find our identity and discover a sense of direction. After his baptism, 'Jesus was led up by the Spirit into the wilderness to be tempted by the devil' (Matthew 4:1). It was there that he wrestled with the implications of his calling as the Messiah and worked out the style of his future ministry. All three temptations revolved around the methods he would use to further the Father's purposes. He would not turn stones into bread, for that would be to feed the body at the expense of the soul, and 'one does not live by bread alone, but by every word that comes from the mouth of God' (Matthew 4:4). He would not jump from the pinnacle of the temple just to persuade the crowd to respond in amazement as the angels rescued him. Such gimmicks would have been inappropriate and unworthy, leading to superficial support instead of real commitment. We then read that 'the devil took him to a very high mountain and showed him all the kingdoms of the world and their splendour; and he said to him, "All these I will give you, if you will fall down and worship me"' (Matthew 4:8–9). Jesus refused. How could he possibly have given allegiance to the devil or have used his methods to further the purposes of God?

The temptation of Jesus in the wilderness was an important part of his preparation for ministry. It was the time for focus and self-discovery, for strengthening and equipping. The truths he learned there sustained him throughout his ministry, and he stood by them at great cost. It was only after he had wrestled with the wilderness experience and showed that he could stand firm in time of trial that Jesus was ready for the task that awaited him.

Similarly, the Israelites did not get to the Promised Land quickly. They had so much learning to do. They went round and round in circles, were often limited in vision and sometimes downright rebellious. They constantly drove Moses back to God in sheer desperation. To lead such a group meant that he needed all the help he could get. No wonder it took them 40 years before they were ready to enter the Promised Land. But it was through this time of testing that they discovered as never before what it meant to be the children of God. They experienced the encircling love and care of God, the depths of his forgiveness and the reality of his enabling power. They had begun to know what it means to call God 'Father', and then to move on and fulfil the destiny that awaited them.

We too must pass through testing times in which we discover the wilderness 'within us'. We may feel a sense of 'inner isolation', or that we cannot communicate in any real depth with either God or others. Our self-confidence is shaken, and we may feel locked up within ourselves. If we believe that God is always leading us into new depths of faith and self-discovery, however, we will see these tough times as part of our training.

In his book *The True Wilderness*, Harry Williams helps us to explore such wilderness experiences. He stresses our need to move away from the 'funk-hole of objectivity' into the reality of personal faith. He says:

God can never be the outside kind of truth, the conclusion of a philosophical or scientific investigation. For a cool head and a cold heart never yet led any man to know any sort of love, least of all the love which passes knowledge. Such theological objectivity is an attempt to keep God out, because his love will confront us with our full selves, and we all have our skeletons in the cupboard.[2]

Moving through the wilderness may well be a necessary step on the way to knowing God as 'Our Father'. We realize that we do not come to know him because we have come to an intellectual understanding of his nature and being. Instead we respond to his loving invitation to follow him. This involves our seeking forgiveness for the past and committing ourselves to a new way of life that involves trust and obedience to God's will.

A while ago, a colleague of mine was admitted to hospital with an extremely serious illness. He remained there for a very long time, and on several occasions was almost given up for dead. Eventually he returned to work, albeit on a part-time basis. When we next met, he shared with me some of the depths of his experience. I shall never forget his words: 'It was tough while it lasted, a real wilderness experience, but if I had my life over again, I would go through it all again. There are some things you can only learn on the anvil of suffering!' He knew that the wilderness was not just a time of testing, but also a way of toughening us up, deepening our faith and leading us into growth and maturity. His experience echoes that of Paul (Philippians 3:10–11). Maybe we can only know the 'power of his resurrection' if first we also know the 'fellowship of his sufferings'.

TO THE PROMISED LAND

Since our own pilgrimage of faith might well be like that of Israel, involving a journey through the wilderness toward the Promised Land, I want us to follow the example of Metropolitan Anthony and travel backwards through the Lord's Prayer, beginning with the petition, **'Deliver us from evil'**.

We may begin with a considerable knowledge of Christianity and some real understanding of the teaching of Jesus, but if we are to discover a more personal faith we will have to acknowledge our need. Moses helped the Israelites to realize that their state of enslavement was not just the result of human greed or of political and social circumstances; it had something to do with God. They were experiencing the power of evil, and only God could release them from its grip. It was he who called them to freedom, and he alone who could release them from the authority of Satan. His call offers hope to those sorely tempted to give up in despair. First, though, they must seek that hope as they pray, 'Deliver us from evil'.

For many, the need for faith hits in times of crisis. To experience a horrific accident, the onset of serious illness or the loss of a loved one may make us feel extremely vulnerable. The extreme stress of modern life, crises at work or the break-up of special relationships can lead to a sense of failure and inadequacy. At such times it is natural to ask, 'What's the point of it all?' Dissatisfaction with the emptiness of a secular and materialistic worldview forces us to face up to the deeper questions of life. We wonder why things go wrong, and ask what the future holds. We find ourselves searching for a sense of meaning and purpose, and wondering whether God can help or even if he really exists. Feeling trapped, we long to be set free. Maybe we are beginning to pray, 'Deliver us from evil.'

Although it is distressing and humiliating to be a slave, we know that slavery also brings with it a sense of security. To take the risk of freedom is to enter a state of utter insecurity. It means taking our destiny into our own hands and launching out into an unknown wilderness.

At the Red Sea, the Israelites acted decisively to leave slavery behind. They had reached the point of demarcation between Egypt and the desert, and they moved forward into freedom. Having escaped Egypt, they were, of course, no longer slaves. In just the same way, once we have accepted the salvation that God offers in Christ, we have moved forward. The past is forgiven and a new way of life beckons. This does not mean that we have arrived, however. We may have a lot of learning to do before we know how to be free. The captivity of our 'Egypt' may be behind us, but we have probably brought with us the attitudes, habits and soul of a slave. Our task, as we move through the wilderness, is to find out what true freedom means. We begin to discover the rich resources of God's love and truth, and gradually learn to trust him. We become increasingly open to the moulding of the Holy Spirit. He longs that we should become new creatures, but patiently waits until we are ready to follow him. Although we are dependent on the grace of God, growth still involves our co-operation.

Left to ourselves, we are likely to fall, and so need to pray, '**Lead us not into temptation.**' When faith first comes alive, we often feel a sense of joy and excitement because we know we have found something real and vital. Gradually, though, the initial sense of having arrived is tinged by a growing awareness of our own inner weakness. The besetting sins to which we are prone, and the attractions of our former way of life, loom large in our thinking. Knowing that we have a very real struggle on our hands, we feel a need to pray for the Lord's protection and deliverance.

Having discovered the reality of faith, we naturally want to grow in it. The example of Jesus shows us what it means to be fully human, so the more we learn about him and get to know him, the more we want to be like him. The trouble is that the more we grow, the more conscious we become of our own weakness and immaturity. We need him to give us time to err, repent and eventually get on the right course, and so we pray, **'Forgive us our trespasses as we forgive them that trespass against us.'**

New life demands a new lifestyle. To hold on to the negative attitudes of the past would cramp God's work in our lives. If we really do want to be free, we dare not cling to the fears, resentments, hatreds and grievances that formerly held us captive. Indeed by being unforgiving we check the mystery of love, and shut ourselves off from the transforming work of the Holy Spirit. God knows we are weak and frail but does not accuse, condemn or reject us. Instead he gently shows us how to leave resentment, greed, and bitterness behind so as to move forward to freedom, and to do so in faith and trust.

This brings us naturally to the petition **'Give us this day our daily bread.'** Just as the Hebrews needed the manna to sustain them through their wilderness wanderings, so we ask that God will provide for our bodily needs and meet us in the depths of our spiritual hunger.

Once the children of Israel had reached the Promised Land, they still needed to occupy it and make it their own. In moving on to pray, **'Thy kingdom come, thy will be done, on earth as it is in heaven'**, we are identifying with God's purposes and making them our own. We are committing ourselves to play our part in making the will of God as present and real on earth as it is in heaven.

Now we are ready to pray, **'Hallowed be thy name.'** We are 'in Christ'. We have caught the vision of the kingdom of God, so we want to honour him, not just with our lips but with our lives. We have become the children of God and are now able to call him **'Our Father, who art in heaven'**.

Thus we have reached the mountaintop. We have come to Mount Zion in Jerusalem. Just outside the city wall on the small hill of Calvary, we see the cross. There the Christian life begins. In the Christ of Calvary we begin to grasp the very nature of God, experience his forgiveness and discern the meaning of faith. Perhaps now we can begin to pray the Lord's Prayer in the order in which Jesus gave it. For as we have seen, to call God 'Our Father' is the goal towards which we have been working. But it is not the end of prayer! It just introduces us to a new depth of praying, so that the relationship we have entered can keep on growing and deepening all our days.

FROM BELIEF TO EXPERIENCE

From the earliest days of the Church, new converts were taught the basics of faith as they prepared for baptism. One of the last things they learned was the Lord's Prayer. They recited it for the first time during the liturgy on Holy Saturday, the day between Good Friday and Easter Day. Thus, after their baptism on Easter Sunday, they could use this prayer from Jesus to mark the new stage of faith and life that was just beginning. They had now entered an intimate father–child relationship with God, and so could really pray, 'Our Father...'.

I was born during World War II, while my father was fighting in Burma. My mother tells me that, as a little boy, I was taught to kiss her 'goodnight'. I would then kiss a framed photograph of a man in military uniform and say 'Goodnight, Daddy' to the father I had never seen. Eventually, the war over, my father came home again. Naturally he was enthusiastically greeted by my mother and then introduced to me. Overcome by so much emotion, I pushed my father away and pointed to the picture, saying, 'That's my daddy.' Of course, the picture was but a shadow of the flesh-and-blood person who really was my father, but that I still had to learn. Gradually over the coming weeks and months I became personally aware that my daddy was a real person with whom I had a warm, loving and growing relationship. Although he had been my father for years, I now really knew it for the first time. What I had known in theory had now become reality. The end had become a beginning.

FOR USE IN SMALL GROUPS

GROUP BIBLE STUDY

Read Philippians 3:1–16; 4:4–13.
* How do these verses fit into the life and experience of Paul?
* How do these passages help you understand the Christian life as a journey?
* How would these verses help somebody going through a wilderness experience?

FOR DISCUSSION

1 Work through the Lord's Prayer from the end to the beginning. Start with 'Deliver us from evil', and conclude with 'Our Father'. Discuss each phrase individually. How do you understand it? What does it mean in your own experience? Is it appropriate and helpful to use this prayer as a way of reflecting on the Christian pilgrimage as a movement from evil towards a living experience of God as Father?
2 How would you describe your wilderness experiences? What helped you get through them? In what ways have they helped you grow? What have you learned from them?

FOR PRAYER AND REFLECTION

A prayer exercise

Starting with 'Deliver us from evil' and ending with 'Our Father who art in heaven', take a phrase of the Lord's Prayer for each day and meditate upon it. In your meditation, ask yourself what it means in:

- Your *head* (your understanding)
- Your *heart* (your experience of God, of life, and what you feel about it)
- Your *lifestyle* (how you can put this teaching into practice and so live out your prayer)

Prayers to use

O Lord, take thou full possession of my heart, raise there thy throne,
and command there as thou dost in heaven.
Being created by thee, let me live to thee.
Being created for thee, let me ever act for thy glory.
Being redeemed by thee, let me render to thee what is thine.
And let my spirit cleave to thee alone, for thy name's sake.

JOHN WESLEY (1703–1791)

Almighty and eternal God, so draw our hearts to thee, so guide our
minds, so fill our imaginations, so control our wills, that we may be
wholly thine, utterly dedicated unto thee; and then use us, we pray
thee, as thou wilt, but always to thy glory and the welfare of thy
people; through our Lord and Saviour Jesus Christ.

ARCHBISHOP WILLIAM TEMPLE (1881–1944)

Chapter 3

'OUR FATHER WHO ART IN HEAVEN'

FOCUS ON THE FATHER

So often we rush into prayer, immediately unloading all our problems on God, sharing our needs and asking him to sort out some mess or other. Indeed we can focus so much on our troubles that we hardly think of God at all. We churn over our problems in such a way that we finish up feeling even more anxious and worried than when we began to pray. 'What's the point?' we ask. 'It's no good praying. It just makes me feel worse.'

If such an approach were all there was to prayer, then such questions would be more than justified. As we begin to grow in the life of prayer, however, we discover how unwise it is to start with our problems. After all, God is not just a 'celestial cleaner-up of messes and sorter-out of wants'. He is our loving God and Father, and it is as we focus on him that we find the resources to cope. As we dwell on his love and strength we are able to put everything into perspective, and we find our priorities turned inside out. We discover that he is with us in our difficulties, giving us an inner peace and serenity that not only strengthens but enables us both to cope and to conquer.

Adoration is always at the heart of prayer. We begin as we focus on God, thanking him for his goodness and reflecting on his nature and perfect will. It is only then that we are ready to bring our particular concerns and hold them in the orbit of his loving presence. This is certainly the pattern of the Lord's Prayer. It is not until we are halfway through it that we pray for daily bread and seek forgiveness and protection from evil.

The nature of adoration, and the need for all of our prayer and worship to be centred on God, is clearly stressed in these words of Archbishop William Temple:

Worship is the submission of all our nature to God. It is the quickening of conscience by his holiness; the nourishment of the mind with his truth; the purifying of the imagination by his beauty; the opening of the heart to his love; the surrender of the will to his purpose—and all of this is gathered up in adoration, the most selfless emotion of which our nature is capable and therefore the chief remedy for that self-centredness which is our original sin and the source of all actual sin. [1]

It is as we learn to adore God that we begin to discover the depths of prayer and find it to be a life-transforming experience. Thus we begin our prayer as we focus on the name and nature of God, and, following the example and teaching of Jesus, we dare to call him 'Father'.

'OUR FATHER'

For Jesus, the word translated 'Father' was not just one among many pictures that he used to think of God or speak to him. It was virtually the only one. The only time we ever hear him using another form of address was when from the cross he cried out, 'My God, my God, why hast thou forsaken me?' That he used these words is quite understandable, since he was quoting from Psalm 22, a moving picture of the soul in torment, crying out to God, expressing deep anguish and yet looking forward in hope. It sums up exactly what Jesus must have been feeling at that moment. The very fact that he could cry out to God in such a way is a sign of the depth of their relationship. He knew that it was safe to pour out his heart to his Father, the one who alone could really understand.

Although it is right to stress the intimacy of prayer and the tenderness of our relationship with God, this must not be at the expense of deep reverence. The Lord's Prayer begins with an awesome respect for a holy God whose name must be hallowed. Following the work of Joachim Jeremias[2] in the 1960s, there is a widespread belief that Jesus taught us to use the word 'abba', the Aramaic word used by children and translated 'daddy'. James Barr[3] has since shown that if 'daddy' had been meant, then the Gospel writers are more likely to have used other Greek words, such as *papas*, *pappas*, *pappias* or *pappidion*. The word actually used in the Lord's Prayer is *'pater'*, a word that many Jews would have used to address God in prayer. The only time where the Gospels record Jesus using the word 'abba' is in the prayer in Gethsemane (Mark 14:36).

Many scholars today would suggest that 'abba' is best translated 'dear father', which is still very intimate. They also suggest that it was not only used by children, but by adults as well. This is interesting, and accuracy is important, but, whatever word he used, a brief glance at any of the prayers of Jesus recorded in scripture will quickly reveal the warmth and intimacy of a very deep relationship. This is an example and a guideline for us to follow.

To call God 'Father' gets to the heart of his nature. He is not some mighty creator who just made the world and then forgot it, but a God who loves and cares for his children and actually wants to have a relationship with them. Through prayer, such a relationship comes alive, grows and deepens. It was the intimacy of his relationship with the Father that so inspired the disciples and caused them to ask, 'Lord, teach us to pray', and this intimacy pervades the whole of the Lord's Prayer. We come to God with the simplicity and trust of a child, opening both mind and heart to an understanding 'abba' or 'pater'.

Ordinary Jews would have found it very difficult to use such an intimate and familiar term as 'abba' to address God. It would have seemed an affront to his holiness and a mark of great disrespect. Jesus seems to have used both 'abba' and 'pater', both of which can be translated 'father', and in using them he communicates intimacy and warmth without losing sight of the majesty and greatness of God. As Dr George Caird says, Jesus 'transformed the Fatherhood of God from a theological doctrine into an intense and intimate experience, and he taught his disciples to pray with the same intimacy'.[4]

Fathers in the ancient world were expected to provide for their children, and so we pray, 'Give us this day our daily bread.' They expected obedience, so we pray, 'Your will be done.' We look to our father for mercy and therefore ask, 'Forgive us our trespasses.' The image of fatherhood permeates the whole prayer and is the key to our understanding of it.

A four-year-old had been told that his father was now a very important man because he had been promoted to the rank of Brigadier. Duly impressed, he asked his mother, 'Do you think he would mind if I still called him Daddy?' The Lord's Prayer ever stands to remind us of the stupendous truth that the creator and sustainer of the universe wants us to call him 'pater', 'father'; or 'abba', 'dear father'; and to enjoy the warmth of relationship that such words imply.

WOULD IT BE BETTER TO CALL GOD 'MOTHER'?

Some today would question the wisdom of using the word 'father' for God. Many have negative memories of their own father. They may even have been abused or neglected by insensitive or over-harsh fathers. For such, the concept of 'father' is hardly the most helpful image to use when thinking about God or praying to him.

Others prefer to pray to 'Our Parent God' or 'Our Mother'. This certainly prevents us from seeing the Almighty in masculine terms alone, but it keeps us thinking of him in personal ways. This is important because he always deals with us in a personal way, and his strength and compassion are always much bigger than any notion of sexuality could allow. In Isaiah 66:13 we read, 'As a mother comforts her child, so I will comfort you'. It is as if we are being encouraged to crawl into a mother's lap to receive strength, healing and love. A similar image, which has a definitely maternal feel about it, is found in Hosea 11:1–4. In this passage, the heart of God aches because in spite of the depth of his loving care, his people have still rejected him in favour of idol worship.

When Israel was a child, I loved him,
and out of Egypt I called my son.
The more I called them,
the more they went from me;
they kept sacrificing to the Baals,
and offering incense to idols.
Yet it was I who taught Ephraim to walk,
I took them up in my arms;
but they did not know that I healed them.
I led them with cords of human kindness,
with bands of love.
I was to them like those
who lift infants to their cheeks.
I bent down to them and fed them.

We certainly need to recognize that in very many ways God is like a mother. This is especially seen in his appreciation of our fragility and the depth of his caring for us. Our real problem is the inadequacy of human language. How do you 'express the inexpressible'? Mere words are never adequate to describe God, but what else do we have? Our notions of masculinity and femininity are hardly appropriate concepts with which to plumb the mystery of God, but we cannot speak of him in personal terms without using them. I find it helpful to speak of God in masculine terms because I want to be faithful to the revelation of God in scripture and loyal to the ways in which God would have been spoken of in biblical times. However, I recognize the validity of the questions and concerns raised by feminist writers, and know that to change the way we address God could well open us to a bigger appreciation of him than could ever be contained in any narrow understanding of masculinity.

THE PROBLEM OF SUFFERING

For many, though, the real issue is deeper still. When we look at the enormous problems facing humanity, consider the reality of suffering, or are perplexed by the power of evil in the world, it is very tempting to doubt whether God exists at all. At times we wonder if we can honestly speak of a God who actually cares or has the power to do anything to help us in time of trouble or need. We are bound to ask if we are not just kidding ourselves. Are we not guilty of turning a blind eye to the realities of life by pretending that at the heart of the universe there is a benign deity who wants us to call him 'Father'?

Aware of such valid questions, we must remember that Jesus called God 'Father' against the harsh realities of life as a poor peasant in an occupied territory some 2,000 years ago. It was a cruel world, and Rome would stop at nothing to ensure the obedience of its subjects. While still a boy, Jesus would have seen many crucifixions and no doubt been horrified by them. He knew life was tough and that to challenge the authorities was an extremely dangerous thing to do. Nevertheless, it was the conviction that God really was 'Our Father' that enabled him to 'set his face to go to Jerusalem' (Luke 9:51). He did so with great courage, for he knew that when he got there he would personally face the horror of cruel suffering and the terror of an agonizing death.

Life has always been tough, and it still is. The fact that we approach our problems and difficulties with faith does not mean that they will simply disappear. Nor does the Bible promise that they will. Instead it tells of a God who, in Jesus, identifies with us in our suffering. Indeed, he cares enough to take it upon himself and bear it on the cross in the sure hope of resurrection.

A few years ago, I visited the burial place of Martin Luther King in Atlanta, Georgia, and bought a postcard containing some of his inspiring words. It reads, 'When our days become dreary with low hovering clouds and our nights become darker than a thousand midnights, let us remember that there is a great benign power in the universe whose name is God, and he is able to make a way out of no way, and transform dark yesterdays into bright tomorrows'. Of course the difficult times will come, but we can take heart, for strength is given and God does see us through.

THE PRODIGAL SON

As a teenager, I used to help in the Sunday school at our church. One day the departmental leader asked the children why we called God 'Father'. It was six-year-old Michael who immediately replied: 'Because when your dad's his very goodest, he's just a little bit like God.' He got it the right way round. All human fathers are judged and fall short when measured against the perfection of God. He is not like our father, or even our mother, for that matter. It is rather we human parents who should seek to be more like God. It is we who should base our understanding of human fatherhood on the ideal of parenthood that we see in God alone.

Perhaps the best picture of God as Father is seen in the parable of the prodigal son (Luke 15:11–32). The word 'prodigal' means 'lavish', a word that certainly described the extravagant lifestyle of the young man who squandered his inheritance. Even better, it describes the extravagant love the father lavished upon him, and really this is the subject of the parable.

A father had two sons, the younger of whom longed to be free. Like most rebellious teenagers, he had to make his own mistakes and grow up in his own way. He managed to persuade his father to give him the money he would eventually inherit, so that he could leave home and make his own way in the world. Thinking he would find freedom in sin, he lived extravagantly and increasingly became a slave to debauchery. When the money ran out, he was forced to make a living by keeping pigs. No self-respecting Jew would ever consider taking such work, since the pig was regarded as an unclean animal. Realizing he had sunk to the depths, and feeling desperately hungry, he decided to go home. He hoped that perhaps his father might be prevailed upon to employ him as a slave. At least he would then have a roof over his head and enough food to eat. Carefully he prepared his speech. 'Father, I have sinned against heaven and before you; I am no longer worthy to be called your son; treat me like one of your hired hands' (vv. 18–19). Imagine his surprise and joy as he saw the father come running towards him.

This story would really have shocked those who heard it. Such undeserved love was just too good to be true. Jewish fathers were treated with great respect. They virtually had the power of life and death over their children. For the son to ask for his inheritance early was in effect saying to his father, 'I wish you were dead.' No Jew could imagine a father being prepared to forgive such an insult, let alone long for his son's return. The climax of the story is seen when the father does what no contemporary Jewish father would ever do. Recognizing his son from afar, he throws all dignity aside and actually runs to meet him. He puts a ring on his finger (the sign of his sonship) and a robe on his shoulders. He then throws a celebration party, showing just how complete is the restoration of their relationship, 'for this son of mine was dead and is alive again; he was lost and is found!' (v. 24).

It is not surprising that the elder brother was furious. In many ways he represented the Jews, particularly their leaders. The story begins as Luke contrasts the fact that tax collectors and sinners were coming to hear Jesus, whereas the Pharisees and scribes were grumbling that Jesus not only welcomed such unworthy sinners, he even ate with them (Luke 15:1–2). The way of the Father was the way of grace and love, but the way of the elder brother was all about rules and duty. It had no room for forgiveness. Eventually, of course, the elder brother would receive his reward. On his father's death he would inherit all the wealth that remained. Since the younger son had already taken his share, the elder had nothing to lose by welcoming the prodigal back into the family. For him, though, religion had little to do with grace; it was a matter of keeping the law. As far as he was concerned, those who disobeyed deserved punishment and not forgiveness. Alas, by continuing to hold such a mistaken view, he missed everything in life that really mattered.

To ponder the prodigal love of such a father is to contemplate the very nature of God. Although one of the greatest storytellers who ever lived, Jesus did not teach just with parables, nor even with words alone. Rather, he taught by example. On the cross he showed just how far God was prepared to go that we might make his love our own and be transformed by it. Perhaps we all have to leave behind our childish misconceptions of God, so that we can find him all over again. Maybe the way to such discovery is really to pray the Lord's Prayer and, in so doing, discern what it means to know God as 'Our Father who art in heaven'.

THE FAMILY PRAYER

We had come from all over the world to attend an international conference. Many different languages were being spoken, and several of them were included in our closing worship. In spite of our different backgrounds and limited understanding, we were united in faith and worship, but this did not really come home to us until we joined in the Lord's Prayer. We each prayed in our own language, and as we did so, we felt a real sense of togetherness. Somehow all our differences faded into insignificance, and we knew that we belonged to each other.

Although in Luke's Gospel the prayer is addressed to 'Father', in Matthew it is to 'Our Father'. The Church has taken over Matthew's form in its worship for a very important reason. We do not pray alone. In both Gospels, the personal pronouns are all plural. Never once is the word 'me' or 'I' used. From the first moment we say, 'Our Father', we have a sense of belonging. We join our prayers with those of the whole family of God. Barriers are broken down and, no matter what our background, all come equally to our universal Father.

This takes us to the heart of what it means to be human, for we were created as relational beings. We need God and we need each other. Being a Christian is tough, too tough to go it alone. We pray, therefore, as part of a universal Church. In so doing, we are in communion both with God and each other. This is why we are 'never less alone than when we pray in secret'.

In the Solomon Islands in the South Pacific, many of the people speak Pidgin English. They begin the Lord's Prayer with the words, 'Papa bilong yumifella'. Our Father belongs to you, to me, and to all people. Nobody can approach God as if he were an 'only child'. Instead, we come together as brothers and sisters, children of the same Father, all belonging to each other.

In our prayers, therefore, we cannot despise our fellows. Nor can we ignore human need by escaping into some esoteric spiritual realm. Instead, our prayers should spur us into action as we seek to hallow his name by living out the prayer, 'Thy kingdom come, thy will be done on earth as it is in heaven'.

'WHO ART IN HEAVEN'

In adding these words, Matthew gives another dimension to our understanding of the Fatherhood of God. He is not some vague, sentimental, generalized and pantheistic presence. By locating him in heaven, we recognize that he has a distinct identity. This reference to heaven is not so much saying 'where' God is, but rather 'who'. As Willimon and Hauerwas have said, God is 'not an ephemeral presence who may have set the whole thing in motion, and then slips into eternal elusiveness. God chooses to be located within, not aloof from his created order. He stands over against us in order to stand with us.'[5]

To pray 'Our Father' gives a sense of intimacy, but to add 'who art in heaven' gives confidence. Heaven is the place where God's will is done and his reign is acknowledged. It is the place of perfection. Our God is the perfect Father. We do not pray to 'Our indulgent Daddy'. The biblical view of God allows no place for such slush or senti-mentality. Because he is 'in heaven', he is the one with supreme auth-ority, the one who can deliver the goods. We are thus able to hold in creative tension the balance between the transcendence, majesty and greatness of God and his closeness and immanence. We enjoy the boldness of intimacy without the danger of over-familiarity.

FOR USE IN SMALL GROUPS

GROUP BIBLE STUDY

Read Luke 15:1–32.

1 Why does Luke link all these three parables together? What themes are similar in each? What are the differences?

2 Consider Luke 15:11–32. Ask each group member to imagine themselves as a character in the story—the father, the older brother, the younger son, the servants. Work in groups of two or three, with each member reflecting on the same character. Imagine their feelings at every stage of the story. After eight or ten minutes, bring the groups together to discuss each character in turn. What have you discovered?

3 In what ways was the younger son lost? Why does this parable speak to so many and touch them so deeply?

4 In what ways was the older brother lost? Why do so many Christian people identify with the older brother?

5 In the light of the story of the prodigal son, discuss the phrase, 'True love is never earned, it is always freely given!'

6 The behaviour of the younger son was most insulting to his father. The Father responded with supreme love. In what ways do you see this love displayed...
   • when the son leaves home?
   • while the son is in the far country?
   • as the son is welcomed home?

FOR DISCUSSION

• In what ways might it be dangerous or unhelpful to refer to God as 'Father'? Why is this so?

• As a child, a young man was abused by his father, and then deserted when the father left home for another woman. The young man now wants nothing to do with his father, but is extremely close to his mother. How would you help him understand why we call God 'Our Father, who art in heaven'?

FOR PRAYER AND REFLECTION

A prayer exercise

This week, make the Lord's Prayer your framework for regular daily praying. Take a phrase at a time, think of the particular things you want to pray for that relate to each phrase, and bring these concerns into the loving, healing presence of the Lord. At the end of the week, jot down some of the prayers you have prayed under each phrase. Then, at the end of your study of the Lord's Prayer, you can reflect on how your understanding of prayer has grown and deepened.

Prayers to use

Eternal Light, shine into our hearts,
Eternal Goodness, deliver us from evil,
Eternal Power, be our support,
Eternal Wisdom, scatter the darkness of our ignorance,
Eternal Pity, have mercy upon us;
that with all our heart and mind and strength we may seek thy face and be brought by thine infinite mercy to thy holy presence, through Jesus Christ our Lord.

ALCUIN OF YORK (735–804)

O Lord our God, grant us grace to desire Thee with our whole heart, that so desiring, we may seek and find Thee; and so finding Thee we may love Thee; and loving Thee we may hate those sins from which Thou hast redeemed us; for the sake of Jesus Christ.

ANSELM (1033–1109)

Chapter 4

'HALLOWED BE THY NAME'

It was on 14 November 1940 that Coventry was bombed. Some 568 people died, fires gutted the city and many of its great buildings were destroyed. Standing in what remained of his cathedral, the Provost, Dick Howard, determined that these ruins should not foster a spirit of bitterness and hatred. Instead the cathedral should be rebuilt as a sign of faith, trust and hope for the future of the world. That dream became a reality, and the new building reflects the ministry of reconciliation in which the cathedral community is still engaged.

Consecrated in 1962, this magnificent building incorporates the ruins of the old cathedral, the stone walls and steeple of which still remain standing. The original roof had gone, its wooden beams burned in the 1940 fire. Those beams are not forgotten, however, for back in November 1940 the cathedral stonemason, Jack Forbes, noticed that two of the charred medieval roof timbers had fallen across each other amid the rubble. He tied them together to form a cross which he set up in the ruined sanctuary. Later, a stone 'altar of reconciliation' was built, and a small, simple cross made of three medieval nails was placed on it. Inscribed on the wall behind the altar are the words, 'Father Forgive'. In a very real way these two words put the whole building in context and sum up the cathedral's worldwide ministry of reconciliation.

In building the new cathedral, the architect has placed a mighty canopy between the old ruins and the new place of worship, holding the two buildings together in a massive statement of death and resurrection. As the cathedral guidebook says, 'To move from the bombed ruins into the new Cathedral building is to walk from Good Friday to

Easter, from death to new life, from the jagged reminder of man's inhumanity to the soaring architecture that lifts the heart.'[1]

It was not just Coventry, of course, but the whole of Europe that was devastated by the fighting of World War II. As the hostilities drew to a close, two British soldiers were walking through the burned-out ruins of a village in northern France. Clambering over the remains of what had once been the parish church, one of them picked up a broken statue of Jesus the Good Shepherd. Surveying the devastation that surrounded him and looking into the face of the statue, he said, 'This is what happens when man is big and God is small.'

When we pray 'Hallowed be thy name', we are asking that God will be big again, that he will take control. For God's name to be hallowed, it must be kept 'holy' or separate. It must be honoured and revered, not just in words but in our actions and lifestyle as well. His name and character must have top place both in human hearts and in the world he loves.

WHAT'S IN A NAME?

In ancient Hebrew, the 'name' of something or someone was extremely important. It referred to the essence, power, character, personality and very nature of the object or person named. It is not surprising, therefore, that the name of God was greatly hallowed. In the Ten Commandments we are instructed, 'You shall not make wrongful use of the name of the Lord your God, for the Lord will not acquit anyone who misuses his name' (Exodus 20:7).

It is interesting to note that the previous commandment forbids the making of idols in any form (Exodus 20:4–6). To describe God as 'holy' is to stress that he is separate from us. He is 'wholly other' and, almost by definition, no idol could ever do justice to one of such majesty and mystery. Furthermore, pagan practice showed that idolatry led to superstition, with religious rituals being used as attempts to manipulate the gods as if by magic. Yahweh, on the other hand, wanted his people to respond to his word with love, trust and obedience. The biblical writers were determined that our understanding of God should not be limited by the images we might make of him or the names we might use to speak of him. This is why the name 'Yahweh' does not attempt to describe him. Instead it emphasizes his being, and the fact that he is the God who acts.

When confronted by the presence of God in the burning bush, Moses asked God to reveal his name. He received the reply, 'I am who I am' (Exodus 3:14). Since, at that time, the present and future tenses were not clearly distinguished in Hebrew, the text could equally well be translated, 'I will be who I will be'. It sounds as though God is saying to Moses, 'Don't try to limit me. Don't capture me in your words, your definitions or your understanding of me. Just be content to know that I exist, and that I will do what I know to be best. I am the God of surprises. Open yourself to me, for there is so much more for you to discover.'

In the light of this emphasis on the greatness and holiness of God, it is not surprising that in Jewish practice the name of God was deemed so special that it would be defiled should sinful lips dare to mention it. The Israelites dared not approach him without reverence, awe and submissive deference, a response no other being could command. Thus it became common practice to use a synonym such as 'the name' or 'Adonai' (Lord), to avoid being guilty of misusing the name of Yahweh.

To 'hallow' the 'name' of God is to give him the unique place that his nature, character and personality demand. It is to offer the worship of our lives rather than just our words. As Calvin said, God must 'have the honour of which he is worthy'. To pray 'Hallowed be thy name' is a way of saying, 'Lord, let me today worship and revere you in all that I am and all that I do.'

HOW DO WE HALLOW THE NAME OF GOD?

First, we hallow the name of God when our worship reflects his glory. The great Protestant theologian Karl Barth described Christian worship as 'the most momentous, the most urgent, the most glorious action that can take place in human life'. He saw it as communion with the infinite, as a living encounter with God. Judged by such a standard, our worship all too often leaves a lot to be desired. We may go through the motions without heartfelt commitment, and our prayers can at times degenerate into rambling words devoid of real meaning. If our prayer and worship are to be real, they must focus on God, and he must remain the captivating centre of our lives and consciousness.

We are taught to pray 'in the name of Jesus', and when we do so, we are not just mouthing words but saying something very profound. We are asking that our prayers should be in tune with the very nature of our Lord and in tune with his perfect will. We dare not, therefore, pray for anything unworthy of him. An extreme example of this was the minister who, following a radio broadcast, received a letter from someone who obviously disagreed with what he had said. 'I am praying for your death', the correspondent wrote; 'I have been successful in three other cases!' Such 'prayers' may well be the workings of a tormented mind, but because they do not reflect his nature in any way, they can never be described as prayer 'in the name of Jesus'.

Second, we hallow God's name when our conception of God is truly Christian. Early in my ministry I worked as a university chaplain. I soon discovered that one of my major tasks would be to help students see that the kind of divinity they had rejected bore little or no resemblance to the living God in whom Christians believed. Only then would they be ready to hear about the God who revealed himself in Jesus Christ.

We cannot behave as though our God is savage, vindictive, harsh or cruel, just waiting to pounce on us if we do something wrong. We dare not picture him as some distant, inaccessible authority figure totally out of tune with the compassionate, warm and welcoming figure that we see in Jesus. Nor may we perceive him as just some abstract philosophical explanation of the universe, divorced from and irrelevant to our daily lives. He is not a figment of our imagination, used to bolster our prejudices, fill in the gaps in our knowledge or justify our pettiness or cruelty. Rather, he is the living Lord, creator and sovereign of the universe. He challenges and confronts us to be the best that we can be, and calls us to hallow his name in all that we are and all that we do. We must 'let God be God' and recognize him as the 'name above all names', the one who draws forth our love, trust and obedience. In so doing, we will 'hallow' his 'name'.

It was the playwright George Bernard Shaw who said, 'God created us in his own image, and we decided to return the compliment.' We may want to make God in our own image, but he is too big for that, and, try as we might, we can never 'cut him down to size'.

Back in the 1950s, J.B. Phillips wrote a very influential book entitled *Your God is Too Small*. More recently, John Young has written one entitled *Our God is Still Too Small*. The title alone reminds us that we still need to pray, 'Hallowed be thy name'.

Third, we hallow his name when our lifestyle brings credit to the name we bear. I became a Christian because of the life and witness of other young people in our church. They had something attractive, and I wanted it! Perhaps more people come to faith as a result of the positive example of Christian friends than for any other reason. Unfortunately, it is also true that the unworthy lifestyle or hypocrisy of some Christians turns others off. Against the pagan background of New Testament times, people needed to see that faith made a difference. The same is true today. We need to show the attractiveness and power of the gospel in an age when so many regard the Christian faith as an irrelevance. It is so important that we 'walk the talk'. If we do not practise what we preach, others will say, 'I can't hear what you're saying, because what you are is shouting too loudly in my ears.' William Barclay puts it this way:

If the Christian is just as likely to collapse under sorrow, if his life is just as frustrated and unsatisfied as the life of a non-Christian, if he is just as worried and anxious, just as nervous and restless, just as guilty of petty dishonesty, of self-seeking, of measuring everything by material values as the man who makes no profession of Christianity, then quite clearly no one will want Christianity because the obvious conclusion is that it makes no difference anyway.[2]

Barclay then emphasizes his point with a challenging quotation from the atheistic philosopher Nietzsche: 'Show me you are redeemed, and then I will believe in your redeemer.'

Fourth, God's name is hallowed when our faith leads to the kind of radical discipleship that touches every part of life. As the cross drew near, Jesus was deeply troubled, and wondered whether he should ask the Father to save him from such a plight. Instead he prayed, 'Father, glorify your name' (John 12:28). The word 'glorify' could perhaps be equally well translated as 'hallow'. Jesus uses the imperative, asking that God should act decisively, and in doing so he recognized the consequences for himself. He was committing himself to that hallowing, even though it would lead to the sacrifice of Calvary.

If God's action is to be sought, it can never be separated from human response. To hallow the name of God demands action, not just words. If we reverence the name of God in our hearts, this must be reflected in our lifestyle. Otherwise our prayers are devoid of all integrity. They have become no more than idle chatter.

We have all laughed at the incongruity of the comment, 'I love everybody, it's people I can't stand.' It is as we move from the general principle to the specific outworking that we begin to realize the implications of what we say. The modern song writer grasps this when he writes, 'Let there be peace on earth, and let it begin with me'. Similarly the hymn writer Kate Barclay Wilkinson (1859–1928) reminds us that the beliefs we hold must transform our whole lives: 'May the mind of Christ my Saviour live in me from day to day, by his love and power controlling all I do or say'.

The God of truth and justice hates everything that goes against his nature. He cannot stand the lies, insensitivity and injustice that taint and spoil the world he loves. We are called to consistent Christianity. How can we stress the importance of family values if we cheat on our partners or fail to give time to our children? How dare we praise the Lord of creation if we blatantly ignore our responsibility to care for the world he made? We do not hallow the name of God if we pollute the land by our selfishness and so hand on a damaged planet to the next generation. We do not hallow the name of 'Our Father' if we ignore the needs of our brothers and sisters. How can we rejoice in God's plenty if we ignore the needs of those burdened with poverty and starvation, even if they do live on the other side of the world? We honour God and hallow his name only when we seek to live completely in tune with his perfect will.

EXPERIENCING AND LIVING THE MESSAGE OF COVENTRY

We began this chapter thinking about Coventry Cathedral. Just as the ruins of the medieval building speak of death and destruction, so the new cathedral is all about resurrection. Above the high altar is the controversial but magnificent tapestry of Graham Sutherland. Entitled *Christ in Majesty*, it reminds us that the risen Christ is also our ascended Lord. He has assumed once more his rightful place as 'King of kings and Lord of lords' and therefore deserves our utmost allegiance.

To attend a communion service at the cathedral is a particularly moving experience. We dare to approach the altar, inspired by the vision of 'Christ in Majesty'. At the foot of the crucifix, which adorns that part of the tapestry just above the altar, we kneel and receive the bread of life. We do so perhaps with the words 'Nothing in my hands I bring; simply to thy cross I cling' ringing in our ears. Standing once more, we turn to walk to our seats, and see for the first time the full splendour of the stained glass. Bright colours on either side of us remind us of the joy and vitality of resurrection life. Straight ahead we look through the plain but etched glass wall at the back, and see the ruins of the old cathedral beyond. The etchings of saints and angels remind us that the life of heaven must pervade our life on earth, for it is in the real world of today that we must work out the implications of our discipleship.

In the ruins of the old cathedral are to be found a series of wall plaques known as 'hallowing places'. They serve as a modern equivalent of the medieval guild chapels that once lined the nave. Each plaque bears an engraving that begins with the words 'Hallowed be Thy name' but ends with an aspect of life in which God's name must be hallowed. One reads, 'Hallowed be thy name in suffering' and another asks that it be hallowed in 'leisure'. Similar treatment is given to commerce, industry, the arts and education. Of course these plaques remind us to pray, but they also challenge the way we live. Faith and work, worship and life are thus intimately linked together. For only when we 'hallow the name' in every part of life are we ready to pray, 'Thy kingdom come, thy will be done on earth as it is in heaven'.

FOR USE IN SMALL GROUPS

GROUP BIBLE STUDY

Read Colossians 3:12–17 and Philippians 2:1–13.
Why is the person of Jesus so central in these passages? How do these readings help you to understand the meaning of 'Hallowed be thy name'? How can we put such teaching into practice?

FOR DISCUSSION

1 Working in groups of two or three, ask the group to draw up a list of the titles of God, Father, Son and Holy Spirit, from the Bible. How do these names help us to understand the nature of each person of the Trinity?
2 Reflect on the following scriptures:
 'Those who know your name put their trust in you' (Psalm 9:10).
 'Some take pride in chariots, and some in horses, but our pride is in the name of the Lord our God' (Psalm 20:7).
 'I have made your name known to those whom you gave me from the world' (John 17:6).
 Why is the 'name' so important?
3 What does it mean to pray 'in the name of Jesus'?

FOR PRAYER AND REFLECTION

Prayer exercise

From the Bible, choose your favourite seven names or titles for Jesus (for example, 'Saviour', 'the Way', 'the Truth', 'Rabbi') In prayers of adoration, take one name each day and focus on its significance. Thank

God for the ways in which we can experience this particular aspect of the nature and character of the Lord. For example, Jesus called himself 'the light of the world'. Reflect on the light that penetrates the darkness of ignorance and fear, protects us from danger, points in the right direction and draws us to itself.

A prayer to use

One of the ways in which Coventry Cathedral seeks to 'hallow the name' of God is through its ministry of reconciliation. The following prayer is used by the cathedral to help in this work. It begins as we recognize that our blindness and insensitivity can cause pain and hurt to others. We therefore seek the forgiveness both of God and our fellow humans. It can, of course, be said alone or with others, and can be adapted to make it especially relevant to contemporary needs.

> Father, forgive
The hatred which divides nation from nation, race from race, class from class—
> Father, forgive
The covetous desires of people and nations to possess what is not their own—
> Father, forgive
The greed which exploits the work of human hands and lays waste the earth—
> Father, forgive
Our envy of the welfare and happiness of others—
> Father, forgive
Our indifference to the plight of the imprisoned, the homeless, the refugee—
> Father, forgive
The lust which dishonours the bodies of men, women and children—
> Father, forgive
The pride which leads us to trust in ourselves and not in God—
> Father, forgive.

Chapter 5

'Thy kingdom come, thy will be done on earth as it is in heaven'

It soon becomes clear to any reader of the Lord's Prayer that each phrase is intimately linked both to what has gone before and to what follows. This is due in part to the love of repetition that is common in much Hebrew literature. Unlike English poetry, which rhymes 'words', Hebrew writing offers a parallel 'meaning'. It says almost the same thing again, but often adds a slightly different picture to develop the idea and shed a little more light on the subject. This is seen particularly in the Psalms. 'The Lord is my shepherd' is very close in meaning to 'I shall not want' (Psalm 23:1) but the second phrase adds a subtle new insight by pointing to the consequence of the Lord being a shepherd to us. 'God is our refuge and strength' is parallel to 'a very present help in trouble' (Psalm 46:1), and again, the second phrase helps us to understand what it means to refer to God in such a way.

The phrasing of the Lord's Prayer is typically Jewish, and the parallelism at this point is very significant. 'Hallowed be thy name' clearly parallels 'Thy kingdom come'. Matthew even adds a third line: 'Thy will be done'. Both the latter phrases can be understood as a commentary on what has gone before. To hallow his name is to recognize God's being and majesty by honouring him both in word and deed. To pray for the coming of the kingdom is to affirm God's sovereignty and to ask that his authority should be accepted. To seek for his will to be done is to ask that his purposes be fulfilled. We are accepting our responsibility to make his will our own, and committing ourselves to work with him in the furtherance of those aims. Each phrase helps us to focus on God and then develops our understanding of him. We move naturally on from his name and nature to his authority and then his will or purpose.

WHAT IS THE KINGDOM OF GOD?

Since the idea of the 'kingdom of God' is central to the message of Jesus and crucial to our understanding of this prayer, it is important to explore what we mean by the phrase. It is worth noting here that sometimes, especially in Matthew, the phrase 'kingdom of God' is replaced by its precise equivalent, 'the kingdom of heaven'. This was conventional Jewish usage because it avoided using the name of God, a name too holy to be expressed. These references to 'the kingdom' appear some 49 times in Matthew, 16 in Mark, and 38 in Luke. Taken together, they present some 50 sayings and parables of Jesus, all of which concern the kingdom. Since the idea is obviously so very significant, we need to look at where it has come from and what it actually means.

The word 'kingdom' is itself misleading because of its geographical connotations. We are not using language in the same way as if we were contrasting the territory of the United Kingdom and that of the Republic of France. 'Kingdom' refers more to the force of rule than to the territory governed. Essentially we are speaking about the sovereign lordship of God over his people and the world he has made. We are speaking of his sphere of power and influence, and of the lives in which he rules. The word would perhaps be better translated, therefore, as the 'reign' of God.

The prophets had long foretold the coming of the kingdom. Isaiah of Jerusalem, for example, looked forward to a time of hope and deliverance very much within the realm of human history. He imagined that God would establish a kingdom of justice and righteousness, which would touch the life of the individual and transform national public life. Established in the Promised Land of Israel, it would be overseen by an earthly king of the house of David.

The Babylonian exile shattered so many of the hopes voiced by prophets like Isaiah. Israel was now a defeated people. Jerusalem had been destroyed. Their kings had been humiliated, and the people had been forced to leave the Promised Land. In the midst of their despair a new tradition developed, which looked for God's kingly rule to come at the end of time and beyond history. It would not come through human effort. Instead it would be established through God's dramatic intervention. The 'day of the Lord' would arrive, when the saviour, God's special messenger or 'Messiah', would come with power and justice to bring an end to the long reign of evil. This 'apocalyptic' tradition is perhaps best seen in the book of Daniel. It was certainly very influential at the time of Jesus.

It was during the time of the exile that a new prophet arose, bringing a message of hope for a shattered people. Known as Second Isaiah, or Isaiah of Babylon, his prophecies are found in Isaiah 40—55. They not only tell of the impending return of the exiles to the Promised Land, but also look forward to the time when God himself will come with power and majesty to bring salvation to his people. He will also come like a gentle shepherd caring for his flock. The long reign of evil will come to an end, and the people will be set free. Jesus knew these prophecies intimately and, as we shall see, he modelled his own ministry upon them.

In the time of Jesus, many religious Jews were convinced that God would fulfil these ancient prophecies and swiftly act to assert his rule. How could the land he had promised to his people be desecrated by the pagan rule of Rome with all its tyranny? They longed for the coming of the day when God would assert his sovereignty.

The Zealots believed that the kingdom would be inaugurated through violent struggle. This is the background to the final temptation of Jesus in the wilderness. He saw the kingdoms of the world from a 'very high mountain' (Matthew 4:8–10), but realized that he could not use the way of Satan to further the work of God. How could the 'prince of peace' use violence to further his cause?

The Pharisees and their followers believed that the kingdom would come only by the keeping of God's moral law, a law that had been worked out in intricate detail by the scribes so as to cover every contingency. They longed for more and more people to accept the rule of this law. Then Israel would experience God's reign because they would be prepared for his supernatural coming. It is impossible to over-emphasize the difference between this view and that of Jesus. His divergence from the Pharisees and, indeed, from so much contemporary Jewish thinking was not just a matter of the interpretation of the law. Nor did it revolve round the methods to be used to bring in necessary reforms. It involved his total understanding of his own person and work. He saw himself as a rival authority to that on which Judaism was based, namely the law.

Any reader of the Gospels cannot help noticing the influential position that these two groups, Zealots and Pharisees, held in the society of the day. But there were other groups, perhaps more ordinary but still characterized by people with an eager and warm piety. They took a less rigid position. In the early chapters of Luke, we meet Elizabeth and Zechariah, the parents of John the Baptist. Zechariah praises God that he has 'raised up a mighty saviour for us' who will 'give light to those who sit in darkness and in the shadow of death, to guide our feet into the way of peace' (Luke 1:67–79). We also meet Anna and Simeon, who recognized the coming of the kingdom in the baby Jesus brought to the temple by his parents. Simeon at last felt that a lifetime of prayerful devotion was fulfilled, and was ready to 'depart in peace'. He praised God, saying, 'Master, now you are dismissing your servant in peace, according to your word; for my eyes have seen your salvation, which you have prepared in the presence of all peoples, a light for revelation to the Gentiles and for glory to your people Israel' (Luke 2:29–32).

These groups differed in their expectation as to how change would come about, but they were all united in the conviction that things were desperate. They all hoped that God would take his power and reign. It would be with great conviction, therefore, that both in the synagogue and in their homes they would pray for the kingdom to come in their lifetime, and in so doing use the following words:

Exalted and hallowed be his great name
in the world which he created according to his will.
May he let his kingdom rule
in your lifetime and in your days…

These are the words of the contemporary Kaddish Prayer, which has distinct similarities with the Lord's Prayer. There is a major difference between the two, however. Professor Joachim Jeremias writes:

In the Kaddish the prayer is by a congregation, which stands in the darkness of the present age and asks for the consummation. In the Lord's Prayer the words may be similar, but the congregation knows that the turning point has already come, because God has already begun his saving work. It therefore asks for the full revelation of what has already been granted.[1]

To pray 'Thy kingdom come' is a prayer for the consummation of that which has already been determined. There is a sense in which the kingdom has already come. It has done so in Jesus. We are praying that it may spread, not as a result of human enterprise and activity but as a result of God's initiative.

JESUS AND THE COMING OF THE KINGDOM

When Jesus said, 'The time is fulfilled, and the kingdom of God has come near; repent, and believe in the good news' (Mark 1:15), he was saying that the years of waiting were over and the new age had dawned. As we read the Gospel we can almost feel the excitement of the crowd as they hear him saying, in effect, 'You have wanted it; you have yearned for it; you have prayed for it; you have wondered if would ever happen. Right! It is happening now! This is the time. The kingdom of God has come upon you.'[2] No wonder the news spread rapidly, and the crowds flocked to hear him.

The kingdom had come. The day had dawned. The signs of his reign were present in the work and words of Jesus himself. They were seen in his miracles and proclaimed in his parables. This brings us back to the prophecies of Isaiah of Babylon, which, as we have already said, Jesus knew intimately. In Isaiah 52:7–10 we read:

How beautiful upon the mountains are the feet of the messenger who announces peace, who brings good news, who announces salvation, who says to Zion, 'Your God reigns.' Listen! Your sentinels lift up their voices, together they sing for joy; for in plain sight they see the return of the Lord to Zion. Break forth together into singing, you ruins of Jerusalem; for the Lord has comforted his people, he has redeemed Jerusalem. The Lord has bared his holy arm before the eyes of all the nations; and all the ends of the earth shall see the salvation of our God.

Believing that Jesus made such prophecies the theme of his work, Tom Wright suggests that he took the three parts of Isaiah's kingdom message and set about implementing them—'release for captive Israel, the defeat of evil and the return of Yahweh to Zion'.[3]

First, in telling the story of the prodigal son (Luke 15), Jesus was explaining why he was constantly celebrating the kingdom with outcasts and misfits. This was how captives were being released.

Second, Jesus spoke and acted as if the long reign of evil that had enslaved God's people would now be decisively defeated through his own work. Incorporated into Isaiah's prophecy there are four poems about the 'servant of the Lord' who will be God's agent in accomplishing this task. Wright says that 'the prophecy as a whole (Isaiah 40—55) sets out the promise of the Kingship of God; the servant songs within it set out a job description for how the promise is to be realized. Jesus volunteered for the job. This, he believed, was how evil would be defeated.'[4] I am not too sure about the word 'volunteered', but it is certainly true that he believed this to be his unique vocation and calling.

Third, Isaiah had declared that Yahweh would return to his people with power and justice, yet gentle as a shepherd. Jesus saw himself as the shepherd rescuing lost sheep. He saw himself as embodying the defeat of evil and the return of Yahweh to Zion.

The Gospels make it very clear that the miracles of Jesus were an important manifestation of the kingdom. This is especially seen in the Beelzebul controversy recorded in Matthew 12:15–30. Many people had been healed, and this was seen as the fulfilment of the prophecy of Isaiah quoted by Matthew. It comes from Isaiah 42:1–4, which is one of the servant songs to which we have just referred.

> *Here is my servant, whom I have chosen,*
> *my beloved, with whom my soul is well pleased.*
> *I will put my Spirit upon him,*
> *and he will proclaim justice to the Gentiles.*
> *He will not wrangle or cry aloud,*
> *nor will anyone hear his voice in the streets.*
> *He will not break a bruised reed*
> *or quench a smouldering wick*
> *until he brings justice to victory.*
> *And in his name the Gentiles will hope.*
> MATTHEW 12:18–21

Immediately after this quotation we read of a blind and deaf demoniac (one possessed by a demon) who has been brought to Jesus and healed. The Pharisees accuse Jesus of healing through the power of Beelzebul, the prince of demons. Not surprisingly, Jesus pours scorn on the suggestion that he is in league with the devil. A fierce struggle there certainly is, but it is not an internal squabble within the domain of Satan. It is rather a war of aggression against him. Jesus says, 'If it is by the Spirit of God that I cast out demons, then the kingdom of God has come to you' (Matthew 12:28; see also Mark 3:20–30; Luke 11:17–23). God was clearly acting to defeat the powers of evil, and he was doing so through the ministry of Jesus.

While in prison, John the Baptist heard about the ministry of Jesus and the response he was getting. He needed confirmation that Jesus really was the expected Messiah. He sent word by the disciples asking, '"Are you the one who is to come, or are we to wait for another?" Jesus answered them, "Go and tell John what you hear and see: the blind receive their sight, the lame walk, the lepers are cleansed, the deaf hear, the dead are raised, and the poor have good news brought to them"' (Matthew 11:3–5; see also Luke 7:22). Once again we have an assertion that the miracles are a dramatic proclamation of the kingdom of God, and a sign of Jesus' messiahship.

As we have seen, Jesus did not invent the idea of the kingdom. It had a long history and a key place in Jewish scripture and tradition. The actual phrase 'kingdom of God' was beginning to be used just before the time of Jesus. It would have been both well known to, and popular with, his Jewish listeners. They may well have understood and believed in the idea of the kingdom of God, but in practice God's rule was very imperfectly acknowledged amongst them. Many simply ignored or rejected it, and even in the most faithful of people his reign was only partial. Nowhere did he seem to have a full and complete reign. That is, of course, until Jesus came. Jesus lived a life in which self had been conquered and God's reign was totally acknowledged. In that real and definite sense, the kingdom of God had come. His very presence embodied it. To look at the values, teaching, attitude and love of Jesus is to see the kingdom and discern its character. He was the kingdom demonstrated in human life. The king was among them in the man of Nazareth! He embodied the kingdom and was the Messiah, but he saw that role in terms of the suffering servant of Isaiah, the agent of Yahweh himself. In his actions God himself was directly at work. It was he who brought release to the captives, defeated the power of evil and rescued the lost sheep who had been damaged and ensnared by it.

Since Jesus transformed the contemporary understanding of the kingdom, it is not surprising that it took a long time for the disciples, let alone the crowds, to understand. Indeed Jesus often refused to define his terms too clearly for fear of limiting their understanding of truths that were really too big for words. Instead he spoke in parables. Through them he shared the essence of his teaching. He paints verbal pictures to show how taking the reign of God seriously can transform our lives. He wants his hearers to see beyond the preconceived notions of the day, to realize that God is doing a new thing, and to be open to it. He is inviting his hearers to explore and experience the kingdom. It's as if he is constantly saying, 'Think again'; 'Try a new approach'; or 'Now see it this way'.

In one parable, Jesus likened the kingdom to the presence of yeast that enables bread to rise. A.M. Hunter points out that the kingdom of God is not like the leaven itself, but is like what happens when you put leaven into a batch of dough. Then it becomes 'a heaving panting mass, all motion, bubbles and explosive energy'.[5] It's like a secret force working from within to bring about transformation. On another occasion, Jesus said that the kingdom was like the mustard seed, so small that people scorn it and give it little chance of success, and yet against all the odds it grows and spreads, becoming a great bush. And again, Jesus is like the farmer sowing his seed. It lands on different kinds of soil. The rocky soil resists its power and the weeds try to choke it, but there in the soil it co-exists with evil and, in humble, unobtrusive ways, gently grows until it produces an abundant harvest.

Frequently the parables of Jesus show that the coming of the kingdom creates a crisis. It demands a response, one shown in our attitude to Jesus himself. In him God's reign had actively begun, and the assault against evil had been launched. He is the only one who had done God's will 'on earth as it is in heaven'. He had come to restore a perverted and damaged creation to its original destiny, and we are challenged to be part of that restoration.

The important thing is that we do respond. To do so may be costly, but no sacrifice is too great to gain so great a reward. This is illustrated by the parables of the hidden treasure (Matthew 13:44) and the pearl of great price (Matthew 13:45–46). The treasure is so vast that it is worth buying the field to make it our own, and the precious pearl so magnificent that it is worth surrendering all the other pearls in our possession in order to obtain it.

The disciples watched the example of Jesus' life, and listened carefully. Gradually truth began to dawn, and they understood more clearly. On the road to Caesarea Philippi, for example, Jesus asked the disciples how the crowds and they themselves perceived his life and work. No doubt speaking for the group of disciples, Peter replied, 'You are the Messiah' (Mark 8:29). Jesus then began to speak of his impending death, but this was too much for Peter to hear, and he protested. Jesus rebuked him, saying, 'Get behind me, Satan! For you are setting your mind not on divine things but on human things' (Mark 8:33). The process of learning continued, but it was only after the resurrection that they grasped the message of the kingdom in all its fullness.

With the resurrection, something radically new happened. The disciples were now convinced. They had come to believe that God's kingdom had actually come and his will been done. Prophecies had been fulfilled, for 'in the unique life, death and resurrection of Jesus the whole cosmos had turned the corner from darkness to light. The kingdom was indeed here, though it differed radically from what they had imagined'.[6] The first Christians actually encountered the risen Christ, and this gave substance to their hope that the new age had begun. Death had been conquered and through the resurrection a 'new creation' had been inaugurated (2 Corinthians 5:17).

To be part of this new creation is to live with paradox, however. Although it has already come into being, the ultimate transformation is yet still to come. How do we reconcile these two apparently different ways of understanding the 'kingdom', and how does it affect our prayer for its coming?

THE 'ALREADY BUT NOT YET'

Wanting to introduce some modern worship songs to supplement the traditional hymn book, a local church decided to produce its own chorus sheet. Thanks to a typing error, the congregation was somewhat surprised to find itself being asked to sing 'Our God resigns'!

When we look at life, it often seems as though God has resigned, his sovereignty is meaningless and evil has the last word. Suffering is an ever-present reality, and it is difficult to see just how a gracious Father can permit such human anguish. Earthquakes, floods, tornadoes and other natural disasters cause enormous havoc. Our TV screens and newspapers constantly report stories of war and its aftermath. And if we look in our own local newspapers, all too often we find evidence of injustice, insensitivity, corruption and even sheer wickedness in our home communities.

Perhaps the best way of understanding this in the light of the kingdom is to say that we are living in the days of the 'already but not yet'. The New Testament teaches that we are living in the last days. Many passages in the epistles suggest that the early Christians expected the imminent return of Jesus. In the later epistles this sense of immediacy declines. Nevertheless, they still held to the conviction that, even though it was going to take longer than had originally been thought, the world was moving on towards the 'second coming' of Jesus at the end of time. We therefore live 'between the times' in the days of the 'already but not yet'.

Very often in war a decisive battle is won, and the other side knows it is defeated, yet fighting may still drag on for a considerable time. After all, isolated units or determined commanders may not want to give in. Individual skirmishes and battles may still be fought and won, but in reality the overall victory has already happened. Both sides need to recognize reality and act accordingly.

Since some of the deepest truths can best be communicated through pictures, we turn to the book of Revelation, where we read of a battle in heaven between the forces of light and darkness. The archangel Michael and his angels are engaged in mortal conflict with the great dragon, otherwise known as Satan or the Devil, and his angels. Satan is well and truly defeated, and this leads to a great song of praise with a glorious climax: 'Rejoice then, you heavens and those who dwell in them! But woe to the earth and the sea, for the devil has come down to you with great wrath, because he knows that his time is short!' (Revelation 12:12). We then read that the dragon goes off to make war on 'those who keep the commandments of God and hold the testimony of Jesus' (Revelation 12.17). The ultimate victory over evil has been won, but Satan is fighting a battle of protest that he cannot possibly win, and we experience the consequences.

In the life and teaching of Jesus, the kingdom had come. In his death and resurrection the decisive battle has been fought and the victory won, and in the coming of the Holy Spirit at Pentecost we see the power of that victory. To pray 'Thy kingdom come' is to pray for the spread of the kingdom in the present, as we prepare for and anticipate the future. In Jesus we have seen 'heaven on earth'. What we long for on earth is already accomplished in heaven, so we pray for it to become a reality here. We have caught a glimpse of God's nature. We long for the fulfilment of what we have already seen in Jesus, and pray for his will to actually 'be done on earth as it is in heaven'. In so doing, we are committing ourselves to co-operate with God and so play our part in ensuring that his purposes are fulfilled. Thus we prepare for the fullness of the kingdom which will be found only at the end of time in the glory of heaven.

'THY WILL BE DONE, ON EARTH AS IT IS IN HEAVEN'

While on earth, Jesus embodied the kingdom, and the people could see that God made a difference. After the resurrection it was the Church, the people of God, who were called to be the leaven in the lump of dough. This is still our calling. We are to be a people inspired and transformed by the vision and values of the kingdom, an alternative society demonstrating what the world is not, but one day will be. We are called to be a microcosm of the new community that lives out the teaching of Jesus. Of course we challenge the values of the world, but we do so from a perspective of hope. In the life and work of Jesus, God has revealed the goal of our existence. We have caught a glimpse of heaven, of another world where the will of God is actually done, and so we have begun to understand the purpose of human life and history. Jesus taught us to pray, 'Thy will be done, on earth as it is in heaven'. Thus he challenges us to be part of a movement that makes a difference, to be the people of God who work towards these goals. He calls us to identify with him and co-operate in the work he is still doing. He inspires us to further the cause of love, justice and truth, and so enables us to help people realize their fullest potential. Rob Warner expresses this beautifully when he says:

Just as an orchestra must retune its instruments before they are ready for a concert performance, so every time we pray 'Thy will be done' we surrender ourselves anew to the Lordship of Christ. We invite him to retune our lives, conforming us once again to his priorities and to the imitation of his character.[7]

We certainly need, therefore, to pray, 'Thy will be done', but this very phrase can lead to misunderstandings. I believe it was Archbishop William Temple who said, 'We have turned what was a triumphant battle cry into a wailing litany.' The very phrase sounds fatalistic, implying that when problems come, all we can do is sit back and resign ourselves to our fate. God's will must be done, and we can do nothing about it!

In reality, of course, nothing could be further from the truth. The Bible knows nothing of blind fate. Instead it speaks of a God who loved the world so much that he came in Christ to redeem it and to bring his children a message of hope. Certainly not a wailing litany, 'Thy will be done' is rather a triumphant battle cry. We may live in a 'Good Friday world', but we are 'Easter people'. We know that the ultimate victory has already been won, and that on the cross evil has been defeated. The resurrection is God's loud 'Amen' to all that Jesus stood for, all that he taught, and all that he was and is. His lordship is not just something to celebrate. It is the truth by which we live.

FOR USE IN SMALL GROUPS

GROUP BIBLE STUDY

Read Mark 4:2–9.

1 Why does Jesus use terms like 'seed', 'growth' and 'yield' when speaking of the kingdom? What does he mean by them? How helpful are these images today?

2 How do the various types of soil in this parable reflect our own

response to the gospel? Note that in the West we tend to concentrate on problem soils, whereas the original hearers, many of whom worked on the land, would have been overwhelmed by the abundance of the harvest from the good soil. What does this say to us?

3 How would you relate the idea of the kingdom as the 'already but not yet' to this parable? In what ways is it a helpful way of interpreting the different aspects of the idea of the kingdom?

FOR DISCUSSION

- 'If He is not Lord of all, he is not Lord at all!' Is this just a pious cliché, or is it really true? Does it foster unrealistic guilt, or is it a challenge to Christian maturity? What practical steps might we take in response?
- If we took this phrase of the Lord's Prayer seriously and lived it, what difference would it make to our world, and to our lives?
- How can we play our part in enabling the will of God to be done on earth as it is in heaven, and so further the work of the kingdom?

FOR REFLECTION AND PRAYER

Prayer exercise

'Thy Kingdom come, Thy will be done.' Each day this week, *relate* this phrase to a different area of your life. The following are suggested, but your circumstances might require you to make them more specific and relevant. *Reflect* on the ways in which God's will is being done, and give God thanks. *Confess* the ways in which it is not being done and seek his forgiveness. *Ask* for God's inspiration, strength and guidance, that in coming days his will might be more perfectly done in this area of life. Is there any *specific action* you can take to further the work of the kingdom?

Sunday: In the Church
Monday: In my home and family life
Tuesday: In my relationships and leisure time
Wednesday: In my work
Thursday: In the communities of which I am a part
Friday: In the life of the nation
Saturday: In the life of the world

Prayers to use

Grant to me, O Lord, to know what I ought to know, to love what
I ought to love, to praise what delights Thee most, to value what is
precious in Thy sight, to hate what is offensive to Thee. Do not suffer
me to judge according to the sight of my eyes, nor to pass sentence
according to the hearing of the ears of ignorant men; but to discern
with true judgment between things visible and spiritual, and above all
things, to enquire what is the good pleasure of thy will.

THOMAS À KEMPIS (1380–1471)

Grant, O Lord, that your love may so fill our lives that we may count
nothing too small to do for you, nothing too much to give, and
nothing too hard to bear, for Jesus Christ's sake.

IGNATIUS LOYOLA (1491–1556)

Chapter 6

'GIVE US THIS DAY OUR DAILY BREAD'

A wealthy old man complained to a friend that his children did not come to see him unless they wanted something. 'They never come,' he said, 'just for my own sake.' As we have seen, the Lord's Prayer begins with adoration. We focus on the one whose name we hallow and whose will we seek to do. We come for 'his own sake', to worship, adore and reflect on the mystery of his being. Prayer has long been described as 'the practice of the presence of God'. It is 'all that we are, delighting in all that he is'. Taking time to deepen our relationship with him is important, therefore, but that does not preclude our seeking practical help. Indeed, asking is part of such a relationship.

Of course the old man was sad that his children came to see him only when they wanted something, but he would have been devastated had he found out that one of his children really needed help but was not able to trust him enough to ask for it. That's exactly how God is. He longs that we should come to him for his own sake, but when we do have needs, he wants us to bring them to him as well.

The Lord's Prayer begins with our seeking God 'for his own sake'. In adoration we focus upon the greatness and majesty of our Father in heaven whose name and nature must be hallowed. We then commit ourselves to play our part in building his kingdom by doing his will. In following this with a request for daily bread, we are changing the focus of our prayer from adoration to intercession and petition. Having begun by seeking the face of God, we now seek the hand of God by asking for practical help. In a very real sense, we have reached the watershed of the prayer.

At this watershed, or point of transition, it is worth noting that although it is brief the Lord's Prayer is remarkably comprehensive. In it we see something of the work of each person of the Holy Trinity, and we bring before God our needs, past, present and future.

Remembering that God is our Father, the creator who sustains the universe, we ask for bread that we might live in the present. We look to the sacrifice of Jesus, the Son, seeking forgiveness for the past through his cross and resurrection. By our willingness to forgive others, we find ourselves being set free from resentment. It is the Holy Spirit— God in the present tense, God in action now—who enables us to deal with all that is negative and so helps us to face the future positively. It is to this same Holy Spirit that we look when we ask for deliverance from evil and seek God's protection as we face the challenge of whatever tomorrow may bring.

It is also a prayer for the freedom to live fulfilled lives as the children of God. We seek liberation from all that prevents us from doing the Lord's will and playing our part in furthering the work of the kingdom. Thus we seek freedom from hunger, forgiveness for sin, and the power of God to prevent us from being tested beyond our strength or brought under the dominion of evil.

This petition reminds us that, during the wilderness wanderings, God sent the 'bread of heaven' to the Israelites (Exodus 16:13–35). It was a sign of God's presence with them and his willingness to sustain them after rescuing them from slavery in Egypt. This 'manna', a bread-like substance that probably tasted like wafers made with honey, was given each day to remind them of God's care and provision. Apart from the eve of the Sabbath, when enough was given for two days, it had to be gathered daily rather than being stored up. There is no room for greed. God's provision is for sufficiency, not surplus. Our prayer is for bread, the basic foodstuff and a symbol of all food. It is a prayer for the essentials of life, not for luxuries.

Having put this petition in context, we need to look at it in more detail.

PARTNERSHIP AND STEWARDSHIP

A group of students spent a weekend in the silence of a Trappist monastery. At the evening meal they were quietly enjoying some absolutely delicious bread, when one of the students blurted out, 'Did we make this, or did someone give it to us?' One of the monks answered, 'Yes.'

They never forgot that answer. Although we may work hard to prepare food tastefully, we must never forget that nothing would be possible if God had not first given us the raw materials. From the story of creation itself, God's provision is seen as a partnership with us, his creatures. He is the creator on whom we depend, but we are called to be faithful stewards of his creation and co-workers with him as we responsibly use his gifts to meet our needs (Genesis 1:27–31).

In some parts of the world it is easy to take food for granted. We earn a reasonable income, buy the food we need, and see it as being ours by right, the natural consequence of our labour. Thus we forget that it is God who provides. Perhaps we need to learn from the poor of today, or the Galilean peasants who first heard these words. Although they worked hard to care for their families, they were careful not to take anything for granted, especially food. If they were subsistence farmers trying to eke out a living from the soil, they knew themselves to be dependent on so many factors outside their control. Similarly fishermen knew that they were always dependent on their next fishing trip to keep body and soul together, and so would have prayed this prayer with deep feeling. To pray, 'Give us this day our daily bread' is to acknowledge dependence upon 'Our Father', and indeed upon other people, as together we enjoy the fruits of his creation.

In praying for 'our' daily bread, the Lord's Prayer confronts the individualism of our consumer culture head-on. Our lives are inextricably bound up with the lives of others in the human family. We cannot pray to the Father of all and remain indifferent to the needs of our impoverished sisters and brothers. This is where faith and social justice, prayer and action meet. As we pray, we remember that some three billion people throughout the world live below the poverty line and have to struggle to get their daily bread. Many of them are not just within our own country, but are part of our own local community.

There is, though, a bigger corporate dimension, which cannot be ignored. We are, to quote Gerd Theissen, 'consuming the bread for the day after tomorrow, by plundering the planet and letting the hungry go away empty'.[1] Selfishness has taken over from stewardship, and unless we are more responsible the consequences are likely to be disastrous. Prayer and responsible stewardship go together. Of course our prayer needs to be backed up by giving to Third World charities and the like, but that's not enough. We also have to face the challenge of how we use the earth's resources responsibly. We dare not hand on to the next generation a planet seriously damaged by the greed and insensitivity of this one. Nor can we ignore the need for more justice in the way we organize our global economy. The needs are ever before us, and we must apply our Christianity both to individual and community concerns.

In a culture of over-consumption, maybe we ought to start by praying, 'Give us the grace to know when enough is enough.' Perhaps the Lord's Prayer will help us to desire what we really need, instead of believing that we need what we desire. Writing from prison, Paul says:

I have learned to be content with whatever I have. I know what it is to have little, and I know what it is to have plenty. In any and all circumstances I have learned the secret of being well-fed and of going hungry, of having plenty and of being in need. I can do all things through him who strengthens me.
PHILIPPIANS 4:11–13

It is all too easy to be overawed by the vastness of the world's problems. We feel that questions of world poverty or the pollution of the planet are the responsibility of governments and those in positions of authority and leadership. Feeling powerless, some are overcome by 'compassion fatigue' and do nothing, just hoping that the problems will go away. There is no excuse for this in a democratic society, for we can make our voice heard. We can all play our part in helping to form public opinion, which does influence governments.

To God, each individual matters, and he can use the smallest contribution to help further the greatest work. We live out the big commitment in individual acts of service, and we must not underestimate their significance.

Some time ago, World Vision International produced a poster that asked in stark white letters against an all-black background, 'How do you feed two billion hungry people?' At the bottom of the poster was a small picture of a tiny boy and his rice bowl, and the caption 'One at a time'.[2]

Just as we live one day at a time, so it really is worthwhile to help one person at a time, to do one good deed at a time, and so little by little we play our part in furthering the work of the kingdom.

ONE DAY AT A TIME

In ancient Israel, bread was made for consumption the following day, so everyone had food in the house overnight, which incidentally helps us understand the parable of the friend at midnight, to which we referred in Chapter 1. The neighbour came to his friend at midnight seeking food for his guests, because he knew that he would have bread ready for the needs of the following day (Luke 11:5–8). In praying this prayer, we seek provision from day to day to perform the tasks God has given us to do.

The Greek word translated as 'daily' (epiousios) seems to have been a word invented by the Gospel writers. Origen, the great theologian of the early Church (c. AD185–254) says it appears nowhere in Greek literature, nor was it in common usage in the Greek of everyday speech.[3] It probably means 'for tomorrow', and some scholars think that behind it is an Aramaic phrase meaning 'for today and tomorrow'. In other words, we are praying that we shall want for nothing today and will be free from worry about tomorrow.[4]

Graham was the victim of a serious road accident in which several of his bones had been broken. A friend went to visit him and was shocked to see him covered in plaster, and with his legs in traction. 'How long have you got to be like this?' she asked. He replied, 'Just one day at a time!'

There is here an important spiritual principle. We are called to trust God and live a day at a time rather than to worry about the future. We also need to pray one day at a time, thus renewing our trust in the promises and presence of God who alone can sustain and support us, no matter what comes our way. We need regular prayer as much as we need regular food if we are to remain healthy.

One of the members of my church had been in hospital for several days and was now at rock bottom, too ill to do anything or concentrate on anything. When I visited that evening, she told me she had received great comfort and inspiration from the hymn 'Great is thy faithfulness, O God my Father'. The words 'strength for today and bright hope for tomorrow' particularly moved her. With deep feeling she said, 'That's what it's all about, isn't it? That's what it's all about!' She was right, of course, for God does give us the strength to live one day at a time. Our hope is in God, and we can trust him. We do not need to know what the future holds. Our calling is to move forward in faith and with the assurance that he will go on leading, sustaining and strengthening us. As Cardinal Newman put it, 'I do not ask to see the distant scene, one step enough for me.'

In the same chapter as that in which we find the Lord's Prayer, Matthew records some challenging words of Jesus in which we are told to get our priorities sorted out, and to start trusting in God. As is so often the case, Jesus starts with the ordinary things of life and through them points to deep spiritual truths:

Therefore I tell you, do not worry about your life, what you will eat or what you will drink, or about your body, what you will wear. Is not life more than food, and the body more than clothing? Look at the birds of the air; they neither sow nor reap nor gather into barns, and yet your heavenly Father feeds them. Are you not of more value than they? And can any of you by worrying add a single hour to your span of life? And why do you worry about clothing? Consider the lilies of the field, how they grow; they neither toil nor spin, yet I tell you, even Solomon in all his glory was not clothed like one of these. But if God so clothes the grass of the field, which is alive today and tomorrow is thrown into the oven, will he not much more clothe you—you of little faith? Therefore do not worry, saying, 'What will we eat?' or 'What will we drink?' or 'What will we wear?' For it is the Gentiles who strive for all these things; and indeed your heavenly Father knows that you need all these things. But strive first for the kingdom of God and his righteousness, and all these things will be given to you as well. So do not worry about tomorrow, for tomorrow will bring worries of its own. Today's trouble is enough for today.

MATTHEW 6:25–34

For some, these words of Jesus are an invitation to impossible idealism. It is natural to worry about things, and we all do it. It is important, therefore, to make a distinction between the negative response of 'worry' and the positive and practical outcome of 'concern'. We should be concerned when problems and difficulties come our way, for it is that very concern which, strengthened by faith, can break down inertia and drive us to appropriate action. Anxiety or worry is quite another matter. It can debilitate and lead to panic, which is the opposite of faith and trust.

Years ago I read in a church magazine, 'Worry is faith in the negative, trust in the unpleasant, assurance of disaster, and belief in defeat. Worry is wasting today's time to clutter up tomorrow's opportunities with yesterday's troubles.' It can be like a thin stream of fear trickling through the mind, which, if encouraged, will cut a channel into which all other thoughts are drained.

In all our consideration of enormous world problems, and of the difference between worry and concern, we can gain rich insight from the famous prayer of American theologian Reinhold Niebuhr (1892–1971). He gets the balance right:

> *God grant me the serenity to accept the things I cannot change,*
> *the courage to change the things I can,*
> *and the wisdom to know the difference.*

THE DEEPER HUNGER

Just as the prayer is addressed to 'our' Father, so now we pray for 'our' daily bread. This is a prayer not just for ourselves but for all our sisters and brothers in the human family. The Pharisees strongly opposed Jesus for eating with 'undesirables' like prostitutes, tax collectors and other sinners. To them this was shameful, whereas for him it was a deliberate sign of the kingdom. His choice of friends was a kind of acted parable, pointing to the central biblical symbol of the kingdom as a great festival banquet to which all are invited. To the Jewish leaders Jesus was celebrating with all the wrong people, and it was in response to their grumbling that he told some of his best stories. He spoke of lost sheep being found, lost coins discovered, and two lost sons being confronted by a father's generous love. As Tom Wright says, he was 'reinventing' the concept of the kingdom around his own work and welcoming all comers to a party. He was offering to all and sundry the bread that spoke of the kingdom of God. He wanted to celebrate the presence of God's kingdom in their midst. 'Give us this day our daily bread' means, therefore, 'Give us right now the blessings of the future.' It is a prayer for the complete fulfilment of God's kingdom: for God's people to be rescued from hunger, guilt and fear. It means, in effect, 'Let the party continue.'[5]

To speak of a banquet at which both physical and spiritual needs are met reminds us that in addition to being a synonym for all food, 'bread' is one of the most powerful of all religious symbols. 'I am the bread of life,' said Jesus (John 6:35, 48), reminding us that he alone can really satisfy our deepest hunger, meet us at the point of our need and sustain us no matter what comes our way. Sometimes Christians speak of the scriptures as being the 'bread of life'. They certainly feed us, bringing insight, comfort and challenge which helps us come closer to Jesus. Similarly, when we celebrate Holy Communion, our faith is strengthened and renewed and our commitment deepened. God comes close to us, and we experience his living presence as we partake of the 'the bread of life'.

When he instituted Holy Communion, often known as the

Eucharist (literally the 'thanksgiving'), Jesus took the two elements that made up the standard meal of the ordinary people of the Middle East in the first century. He took the bread that nourishes and wine that quenches thirst and used them to remind us of his body and blood. As we break bread together, and drink of the cup, we are reminded of the cost of his sacrifice and the power of his love. We renew our commitment and receive of his fullness. In one of his greatest hymns, Charles Wesley prays:

> *Come Holy Ghost, Thine influence shed,*
> *And realize the sign,*
> *Thy life infuse into the bread,*
> *Thy power into the wine.*

That is exactly what happens in this sacrament, for through it we experience his living and transforming presence in our lives and are empowered to serve him.

With the inevitable stress upon the bread and wine, it is all too easy to forget the other tremendously important symbol in this sacrament—the meal itself. The Eucharist needs to be understood against the background of its Jewish roots. Looking back, it is an adaptation of the Passover meal, the meal of salvation. This celebrated the liberation of the Jews from slavery in Egypt and the fact that God led them through their wilderness wanderings to the freedom of the Promised Land. It was the meal of the covenant, that special relationship between the heavenly Father and his children which is right at the heart of the message of the Hebrew scriptures. It was the meal that bound them to him in trust and obedience, and reassured them of his constant love, care and protection.

The bread of the Eucharist is also a foretaste of glory, for through it we are enabled to catch a glimpse into the mystery of heaven. This would have been particularly helpful to those early Christians who lived in constant fear of persecution. Like them, in Holy Communion we can look forward to the great feast in heaven when we shall sit with Christ himself, experience the fullness of his salvation and know the sustaining power of his loving presence. This is why in our various liturgies we say, 'We thank you, Lord, that you have fed us in this sacrament, united us with Christ and given us a foretaste of the heavenly banquet prepared for all.'

To pray 'Give us this day our daily bread' is not only to request food and the basic necessities of our physical lives, but also to ask for spiritual fulfilment. We seek the living presence of God to see us through the day, sustain us in the depths of our being and enable us to live out the prayer, 'Hallowed be Thy name; Thy will be done'. As we commit ourselves to doing the master's will, it is comforting to know that when God calls, he also equips. He does not want to leave us alone to flounder in ignorance, but rather longs to guide and enable us through the working of the Holy Spirit in our lives. In this prayer we ask him to do just that.

FOR USE IN SMALL GROUPS

GROUP BIBLE STUDY

Read John 6:1–71.
1 Read the whole chapter through so that the link between the feeding of the 5000 and the teaching on the bread of life are in context.
2 Read verses 25–71 more carefully, looking for ways in which the crowd failed to understand what Jesus was trying to share with them.
3 How does this chapter help us understand the phrase, 'Give us this day our daily bread'?
4 How does it help us understand Holy Communion?
5 Jesus is the 'bread of life'. In what ways can he be said to meet our deepest hunger?
6 Read John 6:66–69. Why did the crowds leave? What is the significance of Peter's reply?

Read Matthew 6:25–34.

1 Imagine yourself sitting by the Lake of Galilee and, for the first time, hearing these words spoken by Jesus. Then, in groups of two or three, discuss what impact they have on you. Try to sum up what Jesus is saying, using just one or two sentences. When you have done this, try thinking of these words addressed to the 21st century. Write down what you feel to be the heart of the message for today. Discuss your findings as a whole group.

2 In the light of this passage, would you agree that 'worry is interest paid in advance for a debt we may never owe'? What is the difference between worry and concern? How do we distinguish between the two, and why is it important to do so?

3 'Strive first for the kingdom of God and his righteousness, and all these things will be given to you as well' (v. 33). What does Jesus really mean? How does it make sense in the world of today?

4 What does it mean to live and pray 'one day at a time'? In what practical situations might this be important advice?

FOR DISCUSSION

1 The following are the words of an unknown Confederate soldier who fought in the American Civil War. How do they help us understand the value of prayer? In what ways are they true in your own experience?

> *I asked God for strength, that I might do greater things:*
> *I was made weak, that I might learn humbly to obey...*
> *I asked for health, that I might do greater things:*
> *I was given infirmity that I might do better things...*
> *I asked for riches, that I might be happy:*
> *I was given poverty, that I might be wise...*
> *I asked for power, that I might win the praise of men:*
> *I was given weakness, that I might feel the need of God...*
> *I asked for all things, that I might enjoy life:*
> *I was given life, that I might enjoy all things...*

I got nothing that I asked for—but everything I had hoped for,
Almost despite myself, my unspoken prayers were answered.
I am among all men most richly blessed.

2 If God is not just a sorter out of problems, and prayer is not a means of manipulating him to do our will, what is it?
3 Archbishop Michael Ramsey said that prayer involves 'learning to bend our wanting to our glimpses of the divine will'.[6] Discuss this in the light of the Lord's Prayer.

FOR REFLECTION AND PRAYER

Prayer exercise

Take an open Bible, a small roll of bread and a glass of water. Arrange them in such a way that there is nothing else to distract you. Use them to help you meditate on these words of Jesus: 'I am the bread of life. Whoever comes to me will never be hungry, and whoever believes in me will never be thirsty' (John 6:35).

A prayer to use

God, of your goodness give me yourself, for you are sufficient for me. I cannot properly ask anything less, to be worthy of you. If I were to ask less, I should always be in want. In you alone do I have all.

JULIAN OF NORWICH (1342–1416)

Chapter 7

'FORGIVE US OUR TRESPASSES, AS WE FORGIVE THEM THAT TRESPASS AGAINST US'

All his life, the old man had been a sceptic, especially about religious questions. Now he was on his deathbed, and friends asked him if he would like them to send for the parish priest to minister the last rites. 'No,' he said, 'God will forgive me—that's his business!'

These words well reflect the attitude of many today who treat sin lightly, have trivialized forgiveness and, when they do think of it at all, regard it as inevitable. 'Once you replace morality with the philosophy that says "if it feels good, do it",' says Tom Wright, then 'there isn't anything to forgive'. He goes on to say that if we still feel hurt by the behaviour of another, our culture suggests that we simply retreat into our own private world and pretend it didn't happen. In such a world, 'I don't need God to forgive me, and I don't need to forgive anybody else either'.[1]

Such ideas are a far cry from the teaching of the New Testament. In fact, they could be seen as a colossal insult to God, portraying him 'not as a responsible Father, but as a senile old grandfather who not only does not treat our sins seriously, but does not even realize we are indebted to him'.[2]

Although the people of our culture might condone the treating of their own personal failings lightly, they can be quick to blame others when things go wrong. To hear some people talk, one would think that everything that happens must be somebody else's fault. The influence of psychotherapy can persuade us to blame our parents and our upbringing. The sociologist might blame it all on social class and the community in which we were nurtured. The economist might focus on the poverty of our background and, no matter what the problem, a cunning lawyer might want to encourage us to sue for compensation. Sin thus becomes what others do to us rather than what we do to them, and whether or not we forgive them will depend on how we feel.

As we reflect on the Lord's Prayer, we discover a far more authentic and satisfying picture. There is none of the superficial 'live and let live' philosophy which we call toleration but which, in reality, is little more than apathy. Nor do we run away from responsibility by putting the blame on to somebody else. Instead we see that 'forgive us our trespasses', 'lead us not into temptation' and 'deliver us from evil' are all concerned, in an ascending order of complexity, with what still obstructs the coming of God's kingdom in all its fullness. Such barriers are a very serious matter. They cannot be ignored or treated lightly since they limit God's will being done 'on earth as it is in heaven'.

Throughout the Bible, not least in the New Testament, we are held to be responsible for our behaviour and warned that eventually we must face the judgment of God. Sin is treated very seriously and nowhere is forgiveness automatic. Constantly we are reminded of the need to acknowledge our guilt, take responsibility for our actions and confess our need for God to forgive us. We need to repent of our sins, which is much more than just feeling 'sorry' for them. It involves our willingness to turn right about and change the direction of our lives. This is possible only because of what Christ has done for us. On the cross he takes our sin, breaks its power and pays the price of forgiveness. Through his resurrection he shows his victory over sin and death, enables us to experience forgiveness and enables us to live a new way of life. This life is sustained and empowered by the Holy Spirit who guides, inspires and leads us forward in the pilgrimage of faith.

On the day of Pentecost, when the Holy Spirit came with power, Peter preached a dynamic sermon, which obviously moved his hearers. Afterwards some came and asked what they must do, to which he replied, 'Repent, and be baptized every one of you in the name of Jesus

Christ so that your sins may be forgiven; and you will receive the gift of the Holy Spirit' (Acts 2:38).

Paul frequently speaks of our need to die to sin and be raised to a new way of life in Christ. Indeed, this picture of death and resurrection is the key to our understanding both baptism and Holy Communion. It is only as we are willing to die to a life of self-centredness and sin, and be raised to a new life centred upon God, determined to live in accordance with the teaching of Jesus, that we are ready to receive the forgiveness that he freely offers.

We have already seen that Jesus was announcing God's reign on earth. Although the people were looking for political and social liberation, he was offering something much deeper. The prophets had always taught that the oppression of the people of Israel and their exile had been brought about by their sin. 'Son, your sins are forgiven,' said Jesus (Mark 2:5) when he healed the paralytic whose friends had lowered him down to Jesus through an opening in the roof. The Jewish leaders were furious, for this was the height of blasphemy. Only God could forgive sins. In offering forgiveness, however, Jesus was saying that the great act of liberation had arrived. The forgiveness of sins was actually happening now. Then, whenever people did respond to his call, he not only released them from the failures of the past but also taught them how to live in the present by a completely new set of values. They were to be a cell of kingdom people. The past was forgiven. They were set free to live for God and their fellows.

DEBTS OR TRESPASSES?

Some versions of the Lord's Prayer speak of 'debts', while others refer to 'trespasses'. This confusion goes back to the Aramaic language where one word stands for both concepts. Some scholars suggest that Jesus actually did mean that they should have no debts from each other, and Tom Wright says that the early Church certainly believed that this part of the Lord's Prayer referred to financial matters. He points out that debt was a major problem at the time of Jesus. Some thirty years or so after his death, at the start of the Jewish war against the Romans, revolutionaries took over the temple and the first thing they did was to burn the records of debt.[3]

In comparison with other analogies for sin and the way God deals with it, the idea of debt cancellation is admittedly limited but still quite helpful. God made us for a purpose. We were created so that we might enjoy a relationship with him and accept responsibility as stewards, to care for his creation. This is, of course, the covenant relationship to which we have already referred in previous chapters. God cares for his people but in return expects of us the response of trust and obedience. Because of our failure to obey the will of God, we fall into arrears, pile up an overdraft and fall into a permanent state of indebtedness. Since we cannot pay, God in his grace forgives us and writes off the debt.

FORGIVENESS IS COSTLY

Forgiveness is not God saying, 'There, there, it doesn't matter.' Sin matters very much indeed. After all, it cost Jesus his life. Sin is, in effect, our declaration that we do not accept the authority of Christ as Lord, and do not wish to do his will. We would rather do our own. The great Scots preacher, James Stewart, called it 'a clenched fist in the face of the Father'. Sin is an act of rebellion, and a moral God in a moral universe cannot ignore it.

If a person we hardly know offends us, it is very easy to shrug off the insult. As far as we are concerned, the person doesn't know what they're talking about. If, on the other hand, a friend or loved one betrays us, we feel deeply wounded. We trusted them, confided in them, and now they have let us down. Having shared so much with them, we marvel that they could behave in such an insensitive way. In short, the more we love, the deeper the hurt and the more costly the forgiveness. The cross shows us how seriously God treats sin, and how far he was prepared to go to show us his love. He offers us forgiveness and the chance to begin life again, but that offer cost him his life.

After a year in an evangelical Bible college, Jim went to serve as a lay pastor in a small mission hall. Some months later, a friend from college days visited him and was somewhat surprised to see a crucifix on the table at the front of the hall. 'Why not an empty cross?' he asked. 'I would have thought that a good Protestant like you would want to emphasize the resurrection. It's usually the Catholics who like a crucifix showing Jesus still on the cross.'

'No,' said Jim. 'I want the people to know how much he loves us, and how much it cost for us to know his forgiveness.'

THE NEED TO FORGIVE OURSELVES

To this day, many Jewish people greet each other with the biblical word *shalom*. Although usually translated 'peace', the word also means total harmony—with God, with each other and with our innermost self. Such inner harmony and wholeness can never be ours if we are conscious of guilt and worried because we know we have done wrong. For all the trivializing of sin in contemporary culture, many do feel uncomfortable and ill at ease because of wrongdoing. Sin certainly leads to alienation from God but it also damages the sinner. We lack the peace and harmony we seek, and need forgiveness.

I once heard a lady in a Bible class say that while we can forgive and forget the sins of our children, it is difficult to forget our own. Many would say 'Amen' to that. We even find it difficult to believe in God's forgiveness because we cannot forgive ourselves. We may have hurt others and perhaps feel a sense of shame because we have failed to live up to our own highest ideals. The past cannot be changed and we don't know what to do.

The plane has landed, taxied to the appropriate bay, and then waits while one man saunters over to place a small block of rubber in front of its wheels. Thus one of the most powerful machines ever made, using some of the most sophisticated technology ever invented, is effectively blocked from going anywhere by a little piece of rubber. Similarly, one failure, weakness, or mistake that we can't seem to bury and forget can prevent us from 'taking off' in our lives. Things come to a grinding halt because we cannot free ourselves from the shame of our sin and failure.

All too easily, we feel trapped by our sins, weakness and failure. We say, 'I can never be free. I try, but somehow keep on failing. That's the sort of person I am, so I guess I must just accept it.' But it's no good dwelling on our failures or wallowing in the past. Rolling in the muck is not the best way to get clean! We need to be forgiven.

We may feel a failure and know that we have let ourselves down. We are not the people we thought we were. We have failed to live up to our expectations and ideals. But to have failed is not the same thing as being a failure by definition. The gospel sets us free from the feeling that we are trapped by past failure. All of us have failed at some time or another and many of us realize how difficult it is to live by high ideals. We know that there is always a battle going on between the good we want to do and the selfish desires that can drag us down. We may feel ourselves at times to be a bundle of contradictions, or even a walking civil war. That does not mean we are failures, however. Failure is not a permanent state of being. It is only a step in our experience. It should be a learning experience that can spur us on to new endeavour. We take our burden to the cross, claim God's forgiveness and rise renewed and determined to live in the power of the resurrection of Christ. The distinctive mark of the Christian is not that we do not fail, but rather that every time we fall we rise again. We may at times be beaten, but we are never ultimately defeated. We may lose a battle, but in the end, with the help of God, we can never lose the war. No wonder the great Methodist preacher Leslie Weatherhead used to say, 'The forgiveness of sins is the most therapeutic idea in the world.'

As we have seen, our disobedience alienates us from God and the persons we have wronged. Forgiveness essentially means, therefore, the healing of the relationships broken by sin. It is not a matter of being let off the hook. There is nothing sloppy or sentimental about it. If you break a leg doing something wrong, even though the sin may be forgiven the bones will normally take just as long to heal as if you had not been forgiven. A wrongdoer who also breaks the law of the land, and is guilty of a crime for which he is arrested and tried, will still have to pay the penalty imposed by the courts, and rightly so. We suffer the consequences of our sin and stupidity, and for that we have no one to blame but ourselves.

True forgiveness takes us much deeper. Whereas sin alienates us from God, the Bible clearly teaches that through his grace, healing can be received, harmony restored and forgiveness experienced. This means that intimacy with him is restored, a broken relationship healed, and we are free to move forward again. Paul teaches that through the cross we are 'justified by grace through faith' (Romans 3:23–25). In other words, we are treated 'just as if' we had never sinned. By his grace, love and compassion God forgives what we have been, accepts us as we are and enables us to become what he calls us to be. We accept this by faith, and thus make our own what God freely offers to us.

Sin also causes rifts in human relationships. When we wrong another person, our relationship with that person is inevitably strained and damaged. Suspicion, hurt and fear replace trust and naturalness. We cannot pretend nothing happened. There has to be an honest facing up to what has gone wrong and why. Only then can forgiveness take place. It needs to be accompanied by a willingness to repair the relationship. This often means very hard work, which can take a great deal of time and effort.

It is, of course, much easier to write about forgiveness and harmony than to put such teaching into practice. There may well be such deep problems on either side of a broken relationship that counselling or other professional help is needed. Nevertheless, a positive and prayerful attempt to seek God's help in extremely difficult situations can do nothing but good in furthering the way of healing and wholeness, even if it does need to be backed up by some additional therapeutic work. Be that as it may, we need now to look more closely at what it means to be forgiving, and why it is so important.

'AS WE FORGIVE THOSE WHO TRESPASS AGAINST US'

As a young priest, John Wesley spent a short time in Georgia, serving as a missionary in Savannah while his brother Charles served as chaplain to General Oglethorpe, the governor. On hearing the general say, 'Sir, I never forgive', John Wesley replied, 'Then I hope, sir, you never sin!' The Lord's Prayer makes it very clear that we cannot experience forgiveness unless we ourselves are forgiving. It is easy to understand, therefore, why Augustine of Hippo called it 'the terrible petition'. It is the only one with a qualifying clause—'as we forgive'—and to this we must now turn our attention.

'*As* we forgive' does not mean '*in the degree that* we forgive'. Nor does it say '*because* we are forgiving' those who trespass against us. This would suggest an attempt to bargain with God. We cannot earn our forgiveness by the way we treat those who have wronged us. Nor do we need to, since forgiveness is an offer of divine grace and is therefore freely given. Rather, it means, 'as we are living in the spirit of forgiveness to those who have wronged us'. Luke's version reads, 'For we ourselves forgive everyone indebted to us.' In effect, we are saying that we have made what little preparation we can to receive God's gift, for we have shown by our actions that we really do believe in forgiveness and want to put it into practice.

Perhaps the best commentary on this aspect of forgiveness is found in the teaching of Jesus himself. Peter asked, 'How often should I forgive? As many as seven times?' Jesus said to him, 'Not seven times, but, I tell you, seventy-seven times' (Matthew 18:21–22). In the Bible, the number seven represented completeness. In saying 'seventy-seven times', Jesus went much further. He took forgiveness out of the realm of the legal and the calculated by teaching that we should forgive until we have lost count. He then told the parable of the unforgiving servant (Matthew 18:21–35). A slave owed his king a vast sum of money, but as he could not pay it, the king forgave him. The slave then went out and saw a fellow slave who owed him a small sum of money. He insisted on payment and, because this was not forthcoming, threw him into prison. Hearing this, the king summoned him and said:

'You wicked slave, I forgave you all that debt because you pleaded with me. Should you not have had mercy on your fellow slave, as I had mercy on you?' And in anger his lord handed him over to be tortured until he would pay his entire debt. So my heavenly Father will also do to every one of you, if you do not forgive your brother or sister from your heart. (vv. 32–35)

Once again we see how prayer and action go together. Similarly our relationship with God must affect our relationships with our fellow humans, and vice versa. Having received the forgiveness of God for our own sin, we recognize our own fallibility and know that we have no right to expect perfection from others. Just as the forgiveness we have received from God has helped rebuild our lives, so our willingness to forgive others can help rebuild theirs. Dependent upon the free grace of God ourselves, we are called to share grace with others, and that inevitably involves the practice of forgiveness.

A small boy, learning the Lord's Prayer, was heard to pray, 'Forgive us our debts as we forgive those who are dead against us.' He may well have been praying far more perceptively than he could ever have realized. When people wrong us, we do feel they are 'dead against us', and the deeper the hurt, the harder it is to forgive. If forgiveness were easy, however, it would not have needed such a prominent place in the Lord's Prayer.

A deeply committed Christian had been the victim of a great injustice, and was deeply hurt. Knowing this, a medical doctor who was a member of the same church visited her. The doctor listened as his friend shared something of the pain she still felt so strongly. He then said, 'You really have been wronged, and you didn't deserve it, but the most important thing is that you forgive him. You must do so, not just for his sake, but for your own!' Years of experience with hurting patients had taught him that the impact of an unforgiving spirit could have a far more devastating effect on the person wronged than the original offence itself.

Embittered people are their own worst enemies. Negative attitudes in one relationship spill over into others and all too easily diminish our capacity for love and sensitivity. We become cynical as old grievances are nursed and anger and resentment build up. They eat into our peace of mind and destroy all sense of wholeness and inner harmony. By refusing to forgive, we diminish ourselves. Paul says, 'Love keeps no record of wrongs' (1 Corinthians 13:5, NIV). To hold grudges or to nurse grievances, to catalogue offences or refuse to speak to those who have wronged us is contrary to the spirit of Christ. We need to ask God's help in dealing with all such negativity, so that gradually our anger and bitterness will abate and we can discover a more positive and gentler attitude of heart and mind.

Philip Yancey says that if we refuse to forgive, we imprison ourselves in the past and so yield control of our lives to those who have wronged us. He tells how, after the Holocaust, an immigrant rabbi said, 'Before coming to America, I had to forgive Adolf Hitler. I did not want to bring Hitler inside me to a new country.'[4]

Although in our minds we may understand the need for, and importance of, forgiveness, it is still not easy to put it into practice. Indeed, even with the best will in the world, it may well take months or years before we are really able to forgive and forget. Feelings of hurt and pain do not disappear overnight and it is not only unhelpful but also quite wrong to pretend that they do. After all, Christianity is about authenticity and depth. Glib answers rarely satisfy and superficiality helps no one.

Of course it is tempting to hold on to our grievances, cling to the status of 'victim', and wallow in the sympathy that may go with it. In our heart of hearts, though, we probably know that this is not the way of maturity. The good news is that in Christ there is plenty of room for hope. He offers healing for our hurt and help with the often long-drawn-out task of forgiveness.

Forgiveness is not dependent upon our feelings; nor is it simply an emotional response to the situation in which we find ourselves. Our feelings are probably hurt and confused, and may be anything but the right basis upon which to build appropriate action. Forgiveness usually begins with an act of will, but it has to become an ongoing attitude rather than just a decisive act. In gratitude and obedience to God, and following the example of Jesus, we make a determined choice to forgive those who have wronged us. Then we seek to put into practice a positive attitude of forgiveness and love.

There is always a danger that when we become obsessed with the wrongs done by others, we lose our sense of perspective and forget that we also need the forgiveness of God. Our prayers for his help should begin by thanking him for the forgiveness we have received, both from him and, where this is the case, from those whom we have wronged. We should move on to praise him that our experience of forgiveness can help us live with and grow through our weakness and failure. We then need his help to become more sympathetic to others as we realize how strong a hold past experiences can have upon all our lives. We can ask him to help us see things from the perspective of our 'enemies', and gradually, as we are able, we start to pray for them.

J. Neville Ward, who wrote many books on spirituality, suggests that 'our power to give and forgive is often excited and made available to us by compassionate contact with someone else's need to receive grace'.[5] The very fact that we need to forgive somebody else can by itself be an opportunity for our own growth towards maturity.

In the Sermon on the Mount, Jesus says, 'You have heard that it was said, "You shall love your neighbour and hate your enemy." But I say to you, Love your enemies and pray for those who persecute you, so that you may be children of your Father in heaven' (Matthew 5:43–45). Praying for those who have wronged us involves trying to let go of whatever anger and hurt we may feel, so that we can hold our enemies in love and compassion before God. In love we can acknowledge and accept them as they are, and prayerfully imagine them being transformed as they feel more of the loving acceptance of God.

As we continue to pray for them, we also need to take any practical steps we can towards reconciliation. It is impossible to generalize or say what these might be. Suffice it to say that to apologize for any wrongs we have done to the one who has offended us can go a long way towards healing past hurts. To perform natural acts of kindness, helpfulness and courtesy can help prevent the festering of negative feelings and attitudes. To refuse to dwell in the past, to behave lovingly in the present and to face the future with hope is the kind of positive attitude that can help destroy the barriers that divide, and build bridges to further mutual communication and understanding. The important thing is that we make a positive move in the right direction. As Senator Edward Kennedy once said, 'It takes two sides to make a lasting peace, but it only takes one to make the first step.'

Once the apartheid era was over and Nelson Mandela had come to power, a black South African minister met a white man who had interrogated and abused him while he was in prison. 'Am I forgiven?' the white man asked. Without a word, the minister hugged him. Then he asked after another man who had interrogated him, and said that he would like to meet him again. 'Why?' asked the white man. 'Because,' said the ex-prisoner, 'I need to hug him too!'

If everyone followed the 'eye for an eye' principle, observed Mahatma Gandhi, 'eventually the whole world would go blind'.[6] Someone has to break the cycle of negativity so that a new beginning can take place. The Lord's Prayer clearly teaches that we need to be forgiven and forgiving. Only then can we be released from the failings of the past, to face the opportunities ever before us. This involves our being able to stand firm in times of temptation, and reminds us of our need to be delivered from evil. To this we turn in our next chapter.

FOR USE IN SMALL GROUPS

GROUP BIBLE STUDY

Read Matthew 18:21–35.

1 How does the parable of the unforgiving servant help us to understand the teaching of Jesus on forgiveness? How does it relate to the Lord's Prayer?

2 How would you describe the attitude of the servant to the one who was indebted to him? In what ways does this parable challenge our behaviour?

3 In dealing with broken relationships, what have you found helpful? What has been most unhelpful? What advice would you give others?

Read Mark 2:1–12.

1 Why do you think Jesus offered forgiveness as well as physical healing to this man? Why were the scribes so upset?
2 How do you see the connection between forgiveness, health and wholeness? In what ways does this passage help your understanding of this connection?

FOR DISCUSSION

1 What does it mean to experience God's forgiveness? Why is it important? What real difference does it make to our lives? Does the offer of forgiveness from Jesus our Saviour dilute our need to obey Christ the Lord?
2 In 1987 an IRA bomb exploded at a Remembrance Day service. Gordon Wilson and his daughter Marie found themselves trapped under concrete and brick. Marie died, and from his hospital bed Gordon said: 'I have lost my daughter but I bear no grudge. Bitter talk is not going to bring Marie Wilson back to life. I shall pray, tonight and every night, that God will forgive them.' He worked tirelessly for Protestant and Roman Catholic reconciliation, and even met with the IRA to forgive and challenge them to lay down their arms. He lived out the life of love.
   • How does this story reflect the message of the Lord's Prayer?
   • Why has the life of Gordon Wilson touched and inspired so many?
   • How can we forgive without encouraging irresponsibility?

FOR PRAYER AND REFLECTION

Prayer exercise

This week, make the following traditional prayer of Francis of Assisi your own. Note how every negative is transformed into a positive.

Reflect on its meaning, perhaps focusing on a different phrase each day.
Then seek God's guidance as you endeavour to live it.

Lord, make us instruments of thy peace.
Where there is hatred, let us sow love;
where there is injury, pardon;
where there is doubt, faith;
where there is despair, hope;
where there is darkness, light;
where there is sadness, joy.
Grant that we may not seek so much to be comforted as to comfort;
to be understood as to understand;
to be loved as to love;
for it is in giving that we receive;
it is in forgiving that we are forgiven;
and it is in dying that we are born to eternal life;
through Jesus Christ, our Lord.

Prayers to use

Lord, for thy tender mercies' sake, lay not our sins to our charge,
but forgive us all that is past, and give us grace to amend our lives;
to decline from sin and incline to virtue, that we may walk with a
perfect heart before Thee, now and evermore.

SOURCE UNKNOWN, 16TH CENTURY

Give me, O Lord, a steadfast heart, which no unworthy affection may
drag downwards. Give me an unconquered heart, which no tribulation
can wear out. Give me an upright heart, which no unworthy purpose
may tempt aside. Bestow upon me also, O Lord my God,
understanding to know Thee, diligence to seek Thee,
wisdom to find Thee, and faithfulness that may finally embrace Thee;
through Jesus Christ, our Lord.

THOMAS AQUINAS (1225–74)

Chapter 8

'LEAD US NOT INTO TEMPTATION, BUT DELIVER US FROM EVIL'

It was the cartoon that caught my eye. Sitting in his high chair, the toddler had the messiest of faces and the most enormous smile. Underneath were the words 'When I'm good, I'm very, very good, but when I'm bad, I'm happy!'

I well remember, as a young minister, visiting an old lady who was nearly blind, hard of hearing and extremely frail. She was unable to get out very often, so I visited her regularly. After our conversation she would always walk me to the door. I always bade her farewell with the same words: 'Bye now, be good!' Without fail she would reply, 'Oh yes, a chance would be a fine thing!' and then I would hear her chuckling as she hobbled down the hallway, back to her living-room.

Have you ever noticed how many good jokes imply that to behave well is inevitably boring and dull, whereas to be sinful is always enjoyable? Of course it's good to thank God for humour, since it is one of his greatest gifts and adds so much to the quality of our relationships and the fun of life. This, though, should not blind us to the fact that sin is a serious business, and evil is very much a reality in our world.

In the previous phrase of the Lord's Prayer, we asked forgiveness for the past and recognized our need to forgive those who had wronged us. Thus we sought the healing of relationships in the present. Now, as we move on to pray, 'Lead us not into temptation', we ask that God will toughen us up to face the future.

This raises an important question, however. What is the point of asking God not to lead us into temptation? Surely God would never seduce us into sin, so why bother asking him not to? Besides, temptation is such an integral part of human nature that we cannot imagine life without it. The very fact that we are all tempted is part of the glory of our humanity. Unlike robots, we are not programmed to respond automatically in a particular way when challenged. Instead we are people made in the image of God, and thus given the freedom to make our own choices. Indeed, to have such free will is an essential part of what it means to be human.

In Luke 11:4 the Lord's Prayer ends with the words, 'And do not bring us to the time of trial'. The same words are found in Matthew 6:13, but Matthew adds, 'but rescue us from the evil one.' Essentially this is a prayer for protection in the time of trial.

There is, of course, a fundamental difference between temptation and sin. The New Testament goes to great lengths to stress the full humanity of Jesus. He would have had all the normal appetites and cravings of the rest of us, but he did not give in to them. In Hebrews 4:15 we read, 'For we do not have a high priest who is unable to sympathize with our weaknesses, but we have one who in every respect has been tested as we are, yet without sin.'

Humanly speaking, Jesus need not have died. Realizing how dangerous it was for him to be in Jerusalem, he could so easily have returned to the relative obscurity and safety of Galilee, carried on a gentle teaching ministry among those with whom he was still popular, and lived to a ripe old age. This, though, would have been a denial of his vocation. He knew that God had a far bigger work for him to do, but it took him some time to come to terms with the sacrificial cost of his calling. In the garden of Gethsemane we see him wrestling with his destiny. The horror of the cross loomed up before him, and he yearned for release. If God could fulfil his purposes by any other means, he longed that he would do so. From the very depths of his being he prayed, 'Father, if you are willing, remove this cup from me; yet, not my will but yours be done' (Luke 22:42). Here we see the fullness of his humanity, for he naturally wanted to avoid suffering, but we also witness the strength of his character and commitment.

Luke understands the prayer in Gethsemane as a battle with Satan for the outcome of Jesus' impending sacrifice, and in the struggle God sends an angel to support Jesus so that he can pray more earnestly. He is praying that he will not succumb as the temptation intensifies. Of course he would like to escape the cup of suffering, but the only thing that really matters is that God's will be done, and that he should be faithful to his vocation. The Father sees things from a better perspective, and he knows best.

In a very real way, the victory of the cross was won in Gethsemane. Jesus had accepted the will of God, and was determined to fulfil it. His mind was made up, and he knew that strength would be given. Because of the limitations of his humanity he might not have fully understood, or been able to explain how God would use his sacrifice; but because this was the will of the Father, all would be well, Satan would be defeated and the ultimate victory won.

As we have seen from the experience of Jesus in Gethsemane, there is nothing wrong with being tempted, but yielding to it is quite another matter. Just as an athlete goes through a rigorous programme of training so as to give of her best, so God uses temptation as part of the toughening-up process through which the Christian is enabled to grow and mature. We have to choose which way we will go. We have the free will to choose the way of obedience to the will of God, or to follow our own selfish desires. The Greek word for temptation, *peirasmos*, also means 'trial' or 'testing'. This is reflected in some contemporary versions of the prayer, which read, 'Do not bring us to the time of trial'. The point is, of course, that our reaction to the trials and temptations that come our way reveals the measure of our strength, competence and durability. In short, it shows what kind of person we are. In this phrase of the Lord's Prayer, we are not praying that temptations should not come to us. Rather we are asking that when they do come, God will protect and strengthen us so that we do not fall into the trap towards which they persistently entice us.

The American preacher Robert Schuller advertises his television programmes with the words, 'Tough times never last, tough people do'. It is through prayer that our faith is strengthened and we can become tough people. God himself will sustain and guide us, enabling us to face times of temptation or trial without failure. Inner strength is given, new insight is gained, and through the most difficult of times we are led to victory. Doubtless writing from the depth of his own experience, Paul assures us, 'No testing has overtaken you that is not common to everyone. God is faithful, and he will not let you be tested beyond your strength, but with the testing he will also provide the way out so that you may be able to endure it' (1 Corinthians 10:13).

If we are to stand firm in time of trial, we need to be sure of our commitment to God and determined to follow the way of trust and obedience. This means that we need to arm ourselves in advance for the moral, mental and spiritual struggles that will inevitably come our way. Otherwise we will have little chance of survival when we are being tested. Experience shows that sin is not conquered so much in the moment of temptation, but in the long prayerful discipline that precedes it. If our commitment is shallow, we will give up the battle as soon as something more attractive comes along. If our faith is weak, and we are not sure that we really want to be committed to Christ and live a Christian lifestyle, then we will be easily led astray. If, on the other hand, we really believe that God wants the best for us and that the way to abundant life and personal fulfilment is the way of Jesus, then no matter what the cost, we will endeavour to stand firm. That very determination reinforces the commitment and, with it, our sense of meaning, purpose, self-worth and personal identity.

Although sometimes we feel that sin is of little significance, there are times when we are very conscious of the reality of temptation and the enormous power of evil. Whatever our feelings, the New Testament is very clear about the reality of the spiritual battle going on in all of our lives, and warns us to be on our guard. The Evil One knows our weak points, and wants to use them to get a foothold into our lives and so destroy us. In our best moments we aspire to the highest, yet in reality finish up doing what we don't really want to do at all. Paul writes:

So I find it to be a law that when I want to do what is good, evil lies close at hand. For I delight in the law of God in my inmost self, but I see in my members another law at war with the law of my mind, making me captive to

the law of sin that dwells in my members. Wretched man that I am! Who will
rescue me from this body of death? Thanks be to God through Jesus Christ our
Lord! So then, with my mind I am a slave to the law of God, but with my flesh
I am a slave to the law of sin.
ROMANS 7:21–25

Some have interpreted this passage as though it refers to a person who has not yet found the reality of true faith in Christ, with the more positive passages of the following chapter reflecting the joy and power of Christian living. This is too simple an explanation, for even though we may have been very deeply converted, there are still times when our struggle with evil can be very intense. We dare not give in to complacency. It is imperative that we hold on to Christ at all times, or rather let him hold on to us. Only then will we be able to stand firm for what we know to be right.

When we pray, 'Deliver us from evil', we are using the imagery of slavery, and owning up to our need to be redeemed from bondage and saved from the clutches of evil. The good news is that God really can rescue us. When he helps us to withstand our temptations, he liberates us from their grasp and so furthers the work of the kingdom. As the hymn writer puts it, 'Yield not to temptation, for yielding is sin; each victory will help you some other to win'!

An alcoholic was expounding on his problems at great length. The pastor listened very attentively and then gently paraphrased these words from Romans 7: 'The good that I want to do, I can't seem to do, and the evil I don't want to do, that I finish up doing. What a wretched man I am...'. Before he could finish, the parishioner said, 'I don't know who wrote that, pastor, but he must have been an alcoholic like me.' Paul certainly did understand the human condition. He recognized the reality of human bondage, and we would be wise to take his teaching very seriously.

An old Chinese proverb reminds us, 'You can't prevent the birds from flying over your head, but you can keep them from building nests in your hair.' We all have areas of vulnerability in which we are particularly prone to temptation. It is imperative that the person who wishes to stop smoking should spend time in places and situations in which not smoking is regarded as quite normal. To spend all your time with heavy smokers, or to engage in a social life that expects you to smoke, is asking for trouble. Similarly, someone who wants to give up drinking should stay away from the pub, and someone who wishes to slim would probably be wise to stay away from the chocolate counter.

Likewise, if we want to be delivered from the evil one, we should keep out of his way. We dare not go out looking for him, or flirt with him. Nothing gives temptation a foothold more than over-confidence. Realizing our weakness, we must avoid tempting situations in which it is all too easy to fall. Since he has given us free will, God does not force himself upon us. It is only when we acknowledge our need, and really seek his help, that we discover the reality of God's protection and strength. Although it is certainly available to us at all times, we cannot expect God's help if we are determined to make fools of ourselves.

The lion he had worked with for many years attacked the lion-tamer. Recovering in hospital, he reflected, 'I was playing with it, and thought it was only playing with me.' Having given in to a foolish self-confidence and false sense of security, he was caught off-guard. Similarly, if we play with temptation, we will find it plays with us. Very few who commit serious crimes set out with deliberate intent. Rather, their failure comes from a deliberate and, they believe, controlled walk into the field of temptation. This is very dangerous. As Kenneth Slack put it, 'Our betrayal' comes not 'when we are being severely tested in the most obvious way by grief and suffering, but when we are letting our souls take their ease'.[1]

NEVER UNDERESTIMATE THE POWER OF EVIL

In his splendid book, *The Screwtape Letters*, C.S. Lewis paints a picture of a senior devil instructing a young apprentice how to work effectively in the world. He describes his greatest achievement as persuading the world that he does not exist. Certainly popular images of the devil as a comic figure with horns and a pitchfork do not help us. They reinforce a picture of evil that no contemporary person would want to take seriously. We need to find contemporary ways of pointing to the reality of evil so that people are aware of the danger we all face.

The original Greek of the Lord's Prayer can be translated as though evil were an abstract concept—'Deliver us from evil'—or it can be personalized to read, 'Deliver us from the Evil One'. This is a helpful reminder that the most important thing is not whether or not we believe in a personal devil, but that we recognize the reality of evil and take it seriously.

In the closing years of the 20th century we have seen more than enough evidence to convince us of the reality of human evil. The mindless violence and hatred of race riots have horrified us. Mass murder, euphemistically called 'ethnic cleansing', is an all-too-common occurrence. We have seen horrific television pictures of those who have been massacred in Iraq, Rwanda and Kosovo. Similarly we have heard frightening reports and seen many pictures reflecting the evils of civil war. Then, on 11 September 2001, terrorism reached new depths of depravity and caused untold suffering and misery. Hijacked passenger planes, complete with innocent travellers on board, were used to destroy the World Trade Centre towers in New York and to attack the Pentagon in Washington DC. Rightly, people all over the world were appalled at this complete disregard for the sacredness of human life.

Although global in significance, evil is also found closer to home. We all encounter situations of extreme selfishness, heartless insensitivity, cruel thoughtlessness, rampant dishonesty and mindless vandalism. We do not have to travel to the other side of the world to see the reality and power of evil, for we experience it in our own communities and indeed our own lives. Behind the lace curtains of suburban respectability, or the polite niceties of convention, havoc is wreaked in human lives by the selfishness, cruelty and greed that ride roughshod over the needs of others. If ever you doubt the reality of evil, look around you!

The Bible sees evil as a spiritual force of cosmic proportions. It is far more than the sum total of human wickedness, and seems to have a distinctive identity. Dark forces of evil pervert and imprison so many human hopes and dreams, and seem to follow an organized plan to undermine the purposes of God. Paul reminds us of the inadequacy of human resources alone to deal with such a powerful reality. We should therefore:

Put on the whole armour of God, so that you may be able to stand against the wiles of the devil. For our struggle is not against enemies of blood and flesh, but against the rulers, against the authorities, against the cosmic powers of this present darkness, against the spiritual forces of evil in the heavenly places. Therefore take up the whole armour of God, so that you may be able to withstand on that evil day, and having done everything, to stand firm. Stand therefore, and fasten the belt of truth around your waist, and put on the breastplate of righteousness. As shoes for your feet put on whatever will make you ready to proclaim the gospel of peace. With all of these, take the shield of faith, with which you will be able to quench all the flaming arrows of the evil one. Take the helmet of salvation, and the sword of the Spirit, which is the word of God.

Ephesians 6:11–17

This is a picture of warfare, and if we are to win, we dare not underestimate the enemy. Even Jesus, in his great high priestly prayer recorded in John 17, prays that the Father would keep his followers 'from the Evil One'. There is no need to despair, however, for we are not alone. God is on our side. His power is greater than that of the Evil One, and by his grace we can live the victorious Christian life. In resisting temptation we must certainly treat evil seriously, but we need to take God even more seriously.

Such trust in the power of God to sustain and protect us is seen in the following well-known prayer attributed to St Patrick (373–461). Appropriately, it is sometimes known as 'Patrick's breastplate'.

I rise today with the power of God to guide me, the might of God to uphold me, the wisdom of God to teach me, the eye of God to watch over me, the ear of God to hear me, the word of God to give me speech, the hand of God to protect me, the path of God to lie before me, the shield of God to shelter me, the host of God to defend me against the snares of the devil and the temptations of the world, against every man who mediates injury to me, whether far or near.

Although he will never force himself upon us, God is always available to strengthen, guide and help. We may not always realize the closeness of his presence, and sometimes he needs to wait patiently until we have learnt from our own mistakes. Nevertheless, he is always waiting for us to realize our need and so pray, 'Lead us not into temptation, but deliver us from evil'. Then, strengthened by his Spirit, we really can stand firm in times of trial or testing and be delivered from the clutches of evil.

FOR USE IN SMALL GROUPS

GROUP BIBLE STUDY

Read John 8:3–11.
In the light of this story, what can we learn from:
• the attitude of the crowd?
• the attitude of Jesus towards the sinner and the sin?
• the challenge, 'From now on, do not sin again'?

Read Romans 7:21—8:17.
What is the relevance of this passage to our struggle with temptation, and the need for deliverance from evil?
• How accurate is Paul's description of the human condition? (7:21–25)
• What does it mean to live according to the Spirit? (8:5)
• What difference does it make to be a child of God? (8:16)
• What is the difference between the spirit of slavery and the spirit of adoption, or sonship? How does it affect our approach to obeying the law of God?

Read Ephesians 6:10–17.

When thinking about temptation and evil, how helpful is this picture of warfare? Is it really true in our experience? In the light of this passage, what resources are available to help us stand firm? How do they really help us?

FOR DISCUSSION

1 You have been asked by a group of teenage Christians to give them some practical guidelines on how to deal with temptation. How would you respond?
2 Jesus was 'tempted as we are, yet without sin'. Why is this important? Does it have any practical relevance for us?
3 Is there a danger that we think of temptation primarily in relation to sexual matters? In what other ways do we need to stand firm against temptation, at home, at work and at play?
4 How do we experience evil in our lives? How can we be delivered from it? What does God do to help us find deliverance?

FOR PRAYER AND REFLECTION

Prayer exercise

Begin each day by reciting, 'This is the day that the Lord has made; let us rejoice and be glad in it' (Psalm 118:24). Then focus on the first half of the Lord's Prayer, ending with a prayer for daily bread. Thoughtfully share with God your hopes and fears for the day, pray for those with whom you will spend time, and offer each part of the day to God.

At the end of the day, focus on the second half of the prayer, beginning with the need for forgiveness. Ask God to ease and erase the errors of the day, and bless the night hours of rest and renewal. Then offer praise for the day that is past, and trust for the days to come.

Prayers to use

Grant, Lord God, that we may cleave to you without parting,
worship you without wearying,
serve you without failing,
faithfully find you, for ever possess you,
the one and only God, blessed for all eternity. Amen

ANSELM (1033–1109)

Lord, be with us this day,
within us to purify us;
above us to draw us up;
beneath us to sustain us;
before us to lead us;
behind us to restrain us;
around us to protect us.

PATRICK (c.373–461)

Chapter 9

'FOR THINE IS THE KINGDOM, THE POWER AND THE GLORY FOR EVER AND EVER, AMEN'

During the final months of his life, Mozart was commissioned to write a Requiem mass for an influential citizen of Vienna. His health continued to decline, and he died before it was finished. Out of respect for their teacher, his students studied his notes and technique and finally completed a Requiem. When performed today it is considered the work of Mozart, and praise is naturally given to him rather than to his students. In reality, though, it was the work of others inspired by his example, imbued with his spirit and determined to finish the work in the way they felt he would have wanted it completed.

So it is with the final phrase of the Lord's Prayer. Even though these are probably not the actual words of Jesus, they are the testimony of his followers to the style of his praying, the truth of his vision and the reality of the kingdom he preached.

In Luke 11:4, the Lord's Prayer ends with the words 'And do not bring us to the time of trial', whereas Matthew 6:13 adds, 'but rescue us from the evil one'. Such endings would have been unthinkable for the Jews. Their prayers always ended with an ascription of praise and thanksgiving. Knowing this to be the custom, it could well be that Jesus did not feel the need to add such words of praise. He just assumed that his followers would naturally praise God in their own words. Later readers, especially if they did not come from a Jewish background, would have needed more guidance. It is not surprising, therefore, that early in the second century we find that the words 'for thine is the kingdom, the power and the glory, for ever and ever' were added. They are entirely appropriate, since the kingdom, the power and the glory are what the prayer is all about. They get to the essence of its message.

THE POWER AND THE GLORY

The early Christians lived in the empire of Rome, and Caesar reigned in a glory unequalled by the greatest empires of antiquity. His power was absolute, and he held sway over a vast territory stretching from Spain to Palestine and from Egypt to the Black Sea. Contrast the might of Rome with that of the very ordinary people who first prayed these words. The Church was small, and the members usually met in each other's homes. They had little influence in the world. Few would have been leaders of society and many would have been slaves or peasants. The power of Rome would have dominated their consciousness and virtually every aspect of their lives. And yet, with so many forces against them, it was this puny company of 'nobodies' that was able to pray this prayer of triumphant affirmation. And because of the resurrection, they did so with conviction and enthusiasm.

Their Lord had been killed, and all their hopes were crucified with him. It seemed as though once again evil had triumphed, but all this was changed by an empty tomb on Easter Day, the appearance of a resurrected Christ and an inner experience of his living Spirit. It was the deep conviction of these early Christians that death and evil had been defeated and Christ was alive. In defiance of the world, they proclaimed that the kingdom, the power and the glory belonged to God alone, and not to the authorities, rulers and politicians who otherwise dominated their lives.

It is quite obvious, however, that they were redefining the meaning of power and glory. Often working behind the scenes, the gentle, unseen but real power of God was transforming lives, influencing those in authority, answering prayer and bringing good out of the most terrible of circumstances.

In John's Gospel we read of the glory of Jesus, but it was revealed on the cross of Calvary. Some Greeks came to the disciples and asked to see Jesus. On meeting them, Jesus somewhat strangely says:

'The hour has come for the Son of Man to be glorified. Very truly, I tell you, unless a grain of wheat falls into the earth and dies, it remains just a single grain; but if it dies, it bears much fruit... Now my soul is troubled. And what should I say—'Father, save me from this hour'? No, it is for this reason that I have come to this hour. Father, glorify your name.' Then a voice came from heaven, 'I have glorified it, and I will glorify it again.'
JOHN 12:23–24, 27–28

Up to that time, the ministry of Jesus had, with a few significant exceptions, been to the Jews. Now, though, he was moving towards Jerusalem where death awaited him. The coming of Greeks seeking Jesus is deeply significant. They represented the Gentiles. Many Gentiles would come into the kingdom, but not until after the resurrection and the powerful coming of the Holy Spirit at Pentecost. Their seeking him was the sign for which he was waiting. The time had come for him to be glorified, and he knew that this would be costly. Just as in the natural process of germination the seed must die before it can bring forth a new plant, so from his death and resurrection new life would come. Then we would see the glory of God. Good would come out of evil, and seeming failure would be transformed into victory.

In medieval churches and cathedrals, statues of the martyrs were placed at the main entrance to remind people that discipleship can be very costly. In 1998 the Queen unveiled statues of 20th-century martyrs which had been placed over the great West Door of Westminster Abbey. Through this memorial, the witness of well-known people like German theologian Dietrich Bonhoeffer and Catholic priest Maximilian Kolbe will not be forgotten. They were both killed in Nazi concentration camps. Similarly the courage of Archbishops Janani Luwum of Uganda and Oscar Romero of San Salvador will long be remembered. Memorial statues have also been made to honour those internationally less well-known, but still appreciatively remembered in their own local communities—Esther John of Pakistan, Grand Duchess Elizabeth of Russia, Manche Masemola of South Africa, Lucian Tapiedi of Papua New Guinea and Wang Zhiming of China. All chose death rather than to deny their Lord. From different denominations, and all parts of the world, these and countless other martyrs in every age have responded to the violence of the world by offering their lives as a witness to the power of God. Their courage inspires, their faith challenges and their love reveals the meaning of true humanity. For all their human frailty, it is still true to say that in them we catch a glimpse of true sanctity and of the glory of God.

One of the best-known martyrs honoured by a statue at Westminster Abbey is Dr Martin Luther King Jr, the American civil rights leader. In a situation of racial segregation and persecution, he was reluctantly drawn into demonstrating for justice, and gradually became the leading light of a powerful campaign for change. He was a man of prophetic vision, inspired by the Christian call for freedom and justice, and committed to the way of non-violence taught by Jesus and Mahatma Gandhi.

In 1963 he led a national march on Washington DC in which millions took part. A brilliant orator, he will long be remembered for his address to that vast crowd:

I have a dream that my four children may one day live in a nation where they will not be judged by the colour of their skin, but by the content of their character. I have a dream that one day down in Alabama little black girls and little black boys will be able to join hands with little white girls and little white boys as sisters and brothers together. I have a dream that freedom will reign in every state and every city, and all God's children, black and white, Jew and Gentile, Protestant and Catholic, will be able to join hands together.

In the following year, a civil rights act was passed by congress. Change was taking place at home, and international recognition followed in the award of the Nobel Peace Prize, also in 1964. In his acceptance speech we see something of the strength of King's character and the depth of his convictions. He spoke of his 'audacious faith in the future of mankind' and said, 'I refuse to accept the idea that the "isness" of man's present nature makes him morally incapable of reaching up for the eternal "oughtness" that for ever confronts him.'

Against all odds, and in scant regard for personal safety, he held true to the principle of peace-making. When others sought revenge, he called for love. He used to claim that his real goal was not to defeat the white man but rather 'to awaken a sense of shame within the oppressor and challenge his false sense of superiority... The end is reconciliation, the end is redemption, the end is the creation of the beloved community.'[1] Less than a year later, on 4 April 1968, King was shot dead in Memphis, Tennessee. Seemingly he had failed and evil was victorious. In reality a great victory had been won. It was largely because of his work that tremendous changes in race relations have taken place in the United States and, indeed, throughout the world. In his life we catch a glimpse of the power of love, the glory of God and the values of the kingdom.

THE POWER OF PRAISE

Adoration and praise are always at the heart of prayer. We cannot just end our prayer by asking God to lead us not into temptation but deliver us from evil. Rather we need to move back to praise so that we can focus on the God who alone has the power to deliver and strengthen us.

One of the most beautiful prayers in scripture is found in Ephesians 3:14–21. Paul, now in prison, reflects on his calling to be the apostle to the Gentiles. In spite of the deprivation and frustration of imprisonment, he is more convinced than ever of the truth he is called to proclaim. Having given a lifetime of faithful service, he is naturally concerned for the people who have been influenced by his ministry. He does not want them to lose heart because of his sufferings. Instead he prays for them and, typically, the prayer is full of praise:

For this reason I bow my knees before the Father, from whom every family in heaven and on earth takes its name. I pray that, according to the riches of his glory, he may grant that you may be strengthened in your inner being with power through his Spirit, and that Christ may dwell in your hearts through faith, as you are being rooted and grounded in love. I pray that you may have the power to comprehend, with all the saints, what is the breadth and length and height and depth, and to know the love of Christ that surpasses knowledge, so that you may be filled with all the fullness of God.

Now to him who by the power at work within us is able to accomplish abundantly far more than we can ask or imagine, to him be glory in the church and in Christ Jesus to all generations, forever and ever. Amen.

Although Paul prays for his readers, the focus is not so much upon them as upon God. He stresses the vast resources of God's grace, and highlights what God can do for us. Indeed he knows that as the spirit of praise dominates all that we have and all that we are, the prayer will be answered and true growth will follow. Dr W.E. Orchard, a great man of prayer, was well aware of the importance of praise and adoration. He once told a friend that he had prayed for him for an hour the previous day. 'How do you do that?' asked the friend. 'How do you go about praying for anyone for a whole hour?' Orchard replied, 'I thought about God for 59 minutes and then just mentioned your name.'

Julia was bearing the kind of problems no student should ever have to carry. At the end of term, deeply troubled, she came to see me, and asked if I would pray for her. Early in the following term I asked how things were going. 'Fine, thanks,' she said. 'It's not that the problems have gone away, indeed in some ways they're a bit worse, but I'm not worried about them any more. God has given me the strength to cope, and I know he will see me through.' We spoke at great length and found ourselves looking together at Philippians 4:4–7:

Rejoice in the Lord always; again I will say, Rejoice. Let your gentleness be known to everyone. The Lord is near. Do not worry about anything, but in everything by prayer and supplication with thanksgiving let your requests be made known to God. And the peace of God, which surpasses all understanding, will guard your hearts and your minds in Christ Jesus.

All too often when problems come we find ourselves wanting to run away. Quite naturally we feel that unless we escape we will never find the peace for which we long—but the peace of God surpasses human understanding. Instead of helping us run away, it enables us to face up to our problems and find a way through them. As we face them head-on, and then offer them up to God, we find ourselves receiving the strength to deal with them. Rather than being confused in our understanding, or overwhelmed by our feelings and emotions, we find ourselves kept and sustained by the love of God. This is what Paul means when he says that God's peace will 'guard' our hearts and minds in Christ Jesus. As our relationship with the Lord deepens, we really do find new strength to cope, and protection in our time of need.

In wrestling with our difficulties, we find ourselves growing. In the midst of anguish, we discover the power of God. From days of darkness and death, we are led to the light of resurrection. The secret is always to rejoice, and thus experience the power of praise. No matter what problems come, we do not give in to negative attitudes, and there is certainly no place for despair or cynicism. Instead we praise God that somewhere in the midst of our desperation we can find him, and that he will lead us forward to victory.

ON SINGING THE PRAISES OF GOD

Many of the early Christian martyrs went to their deaths singing the praises of God. Such music would have strengthened resolve and built courage. Similarly, an outpouring of music and singing has often accompanied times of religious revival and helped to give it the momentum needed to advance. It is said that Methodism, for example, was 'born in song', and thanks to the magnificent hymns of Charles Wesley we can still praise God in the words and music of the evangel-ical revival. Imagine the early Methodists some 250 years ago. Britain was experiencing an industrial revolution, and the mines and factories were working flat out. Whole families worked long hours in awful conditions and great poverty. Many felt dehumanized, under-valued and exhausted. In the evenings, though, they would meet in each other's homes for fellowship. In these groups, known as 'class meetings', they would explore the meaning of faith, study the Bible and sing the praises of God. They sang their theology, and as they did so they learned their Bibles, discovered new depths of God's love and found their faith enriched and strengthened. Helped by such singing, fellowship came alive and spirits were lifted. Hope was reborn and lives were made new. Since music touches our emotions, it reaches depths within us that words alone could never do.

Singing can make prayer live. When you feel that you can't pray, it is often a good idea to start singing a worship song or hymn. Sometimes the act of singing well-known words can enable us to explore depths of prayer, previously unknown. Praise is medicine for the tired soul. It lifts us out of our troubles and into the light and peace of God's presence.

ACCEPTING THE KING, AND LIVING IN THE KINGDOM

In the closing years of the 19th and the early years of the 20th centuries, there was a strong belief in the inevitability of progress. The kingdom of God, the ideal society, would eventually come, but only if we all worked to bring it about. Times have changed, and the mood of the present age is very different. For all the vast and rapid achievements of humankind, we are extremely concerned about the consequences of our actions. Many are deeply troubled by the impact of regional wars and international terrorism, and see global warming and the irresponsible use of biotechnology or genetic engineering as major threats to our future security. In short, we are less optimistic about the future and less trusting of human ability to bring about the progress we require. In the New Testament, we find Jesus proclaiming the kingdom as the gift of God rather than the result of human effort. Our responsibility is to accept it, acknowledge the lordship of Christ, and then offer ourselves to him in obedient allegiance and grateful service.

Although God does not force his reign upon us, he does long that we should respond to it. His is the transforming power of love, a love that listens and a power that acts. He wants us to be open to the moulding of the Holy Spirit, so that we will begin to reflect something of his love, presence, power and glory. This is not an easy path. As the example of Jesus makes plain, the way of love and commitment is costly, and the 'glory of God' is seen more on a cross than a throne.

It is great that in the life of Jesus we see kingdom, power and glory. The amazing truth is that he wants us ordinary people to participate in the same kingdom. It is as we live out the values of the kingdom that we will reflect something of the king himself. We will find ourselves journeying along the road to holiness.

Of course it is not enough just to pray the words, 'Thine is the kingdom, the power and the glory'. True prayer involves our living as though Jesus really were king in our lives. This is not the easiest thing for us to understand. Kings in the ancient world had absolute power over the lives of their subjects, and so were quite unlike the constitutional monarchies that we know today. Although contemporary monarchs may have all the trappings of power, it is the politicians who make the decisions that matter. Some time ago I read a newspaper article about the Prince of Monaco. Apparently he has more titles than any other sovereign, even though he rules over a state of less than one square mile. The article cynically went on to say that the heir to the throne, Prince Albert, took his duties very seriously until he discovered there weren't any!

All too often we treat God like a constitutional monarch. In our worship we give him all the glory, but the power lies elsewhere. We want to make the important decisions. We want to be in charge of our own destiny. Although we may pay lip service to the lordship of Christ, we conveniently forget that Jesus calls us to deny ourselves, take up the cross and follow him. In other words, he calls us to commitment.

When we pray, 'For thine is the kingdom, the power and the glory', we are saying that we want God's kingdom to come and his will to be done, and that we are willing to let it begin in us. We are acknowledging his lordship, and committing ourselves to live for him. When a couple's marriage was going through very difficult times, the wife complained about her husband's insensitivity. In response he said, 'But darling, you know I love you!' With deep feeling she retorted, 'Don't just say it, live it!' To pray the Lord's Prayer is to commit ourselves to live by the values of the kingdom. We are taking the medicine ourselves so that we can be strong enough to share it with others. We are signing up to play our part in furthering the purposes of God.

In the cross and resurrection, the ultimate victory has already been won. This conviction is proclaimed in the words, 'For thine is the kingdom, the power and the glory, for ever and ever.' No wonder we follow it by saying, 'Amen'. 'This is the truth, so be it,' we proclaim. Thus we are committed to live as citizens of the kingdom, and know that in so doing we will experience the power and the glory for ever.

FOR USE IN SMALL GROUPS

GROUP BIBLE STUDY

Read John 17:1–26.
Some commentators suggest that many of the ideas and phrases used by Jesus in this 'high priestly' prayer reflect the Lord's Prayer, and that he may even have used it as a framework for his own prayers. Work through this chapter and examine the similarities.

Read Philippians 3:4–16.
Here Paul shares his testimony. In his early life he had everything a Jew could possibly want, but now he knew that, compared to the joy of knowing Christ as Lord, all of it was 'rubbish'. Although 'in Christ' he had found so much, there was still more to discover. He therefore uses an athletic analogy, inviting us to join him in running the race of faith. The secret of success is to keep our eyes firmly fixed on Jesus, the goal of all our endeavours. Focus on the following verses, and then answer the questions:

Not that I have already obtained this or have already reached the goal; but I press on to make it my own, because Christ Jesus has made me his own. Beloved, I do not consider that I have made it my own; but this one thing I do: forgetting what lies behind and straining forward to what lies ahead, I press on toward the goal for the prize of the heavenly call of God in Christ Jesus. Let those of us then who are mature be of the same mind; and if you think differently about anything, this too God will reveal to you. Only let us hold fast to what we have attained.

PHILIPPIANS 3:12–16

- In what ways do we need to keep our eyes on Jesus and how does doing so help us to grow?
- In your experience of prayer, how important is praise? How does praise relate to this passage?
- Why does Paul insist that the mature should be of the same mind?

FOR DISCUSSION

1 I once heard a preacher say, 'Praise is the darkroom that changes negatives into positives.' What did he mean? Is he right? If so, how does the change come about?
2 What does it mean to offer our problems up to God? How does this help?

CONCLUDING EXERCISES

Divide into groups of three or four, and try to paraphrase the Lord's Prayer. Then come together to share notes. What are the main things you have learned from this study of the Lord's Prayer? How will it affect your living? How has it helped you to pray?

FOR REFLECTION AND PRAYER

Prayer exercise

Work out how you could use the Lord's Prayer as a framework for your own praying. What particular concerns would you share with God for each phrase in the prayer? Use your framework each day this week and modify it as you go along.

A prayer to use

Thanks be to thee, Lord Jesus Christ, for all the benefits which Thou hast given us, for all the pains and insults which Thou hast borne for us. O most merciful Redeemer, Friend and Brother, may we know thee more clearly, love thee more dearly, and follow thee more nearly, now and for ever.

RICHARD OF CHICHESTER (1197–1253)

NOTES FOR HOME STUDY GROUP LEADERS AND MEMBERS

Many in the church are well used to meeting in small groups for Bible study, prayer and discussion, but for others this is a new experience, so I set out below a few brief guidelines that may be of use.

Groups often work best when they meet for a 'term' with a very obvious starting and finishing date. This book is intended for a nine-week course. Members are then encouraged to come to all meetings, knowing that there will be a break before a new series begins. To keep a sense of progression, it is best to meet weekly, or perhaps fortnightly.

GENERAL GUIDELINES

1 The ideal number of members of a cell group is 8–12.
2 The larger the group, the more important it is to divide occasionally into smaller 'buzz groups'. This will give everybody the opportunity to share more easily.
3 It is important to agree the starting and finishing times and keep to them. Many groups find that an ideal length of meeting is 90 minutes, plus informal refreshment time. Some groups might prefer to be shorter or longer. The important thing is for the group to agree what is right for them.
4 It is valuable to start and end each meeting with prayer.
5 Rather than relying on one person to do everything, it is often good to share leadership roles around the group. This helps the members to discover and develop their gifts.

The host arranges the room and ensures that chairs are in a circle so that everyone can see each other and especially the leader. Chairs focus on the TV in so many living-rooms and this usually necessitates some slight rearrangement if the group dynamics are to work well.

The refreshment co-ordinator need not necessarily be the same person as the host!

The leader prepares the session, fosters discussion and ensures that everyone is involved.

The pastoral carer notices when someone is missing and phones the following day to check that nothing is wrong, visits any who are sick, and organizes birthday or 'get-well' cards and so on which can be signed by all the members of the group.

The prayer co-ordinator organizes a rota of those who will begin and end each session with an appropriate prayer. He or she will work in harmony with the pastoral carer to make sure that prayer requests and needs are shared with the group. Some groups also find it helpful to organize a prayer partner scheme whereby members are linked with each other to pray for specific needs or concerns.

6 Some churches find it helpful to have several home study groups all following the same material. Special sermons can be preached the preceding Sunday to introduce the theme, or alternatively on the following Sunday as a revision exercise. It is also good to have an introductory meeting to give some background to the course. This gives members of all the groups an opportunity to come together, and so deepen fellowship. It is particularly effective when it includes eating a meal together. Small groups can be threatening for those who are not used to them, so an introductory meeting can help to allay fears. Similarly a concluding meeting gives an opportunity for each of the groups to share what they have discovered.

THE PREPARATION

Each member is encouraged to read the appropriate chapter in this book in preparation for the discussion. As they do so, it is often good to briefly note:
• Things not understood, or which require further explanation.
• Helpful insights gained and new light received.
• Practical consequences and new directions to follow.

Perhaps the group could begin by asking members to share with each other the points they have noted. At the end of the meeting you can check if their concerns have been met and questions answered.

If members do not have time to read the appropriate chapter in the book, the Bible studies and discussion questions should be sufficient to foster stimulating discussion in their own right.

Because all groups are different, I have prepared more material than can be used in any one session. *The leader* should therefore choose the questions that best suit the needs of the group and concentrate on them, rather than trying to use all the material given.

The Bible studies are designed to take at least half of the time. The questions are only guidelines or pointers. It is more important to let the scriptures speak for themselves. The questions are just tools to help us explore them.

The discussion questions are intended to provide a suitable follow-on from the Bible studies, and often help us consider other related issues. They are also more 'user-friendly' for those not used to Bible study.

The prayer exercise is intended for members to use at home, but it is usually good to spend a little group time discussing how helpful they found the exercise given the previous week, and how they might approach the one for the week to come.

The prayer to use is intended for members to use at home, but could also be used to open or close the meetings.

THE MEETING ITSELF

A home study group does not need an expert teacher or lecturer to do all the work. The leader should not normally need to give an introduction, and certainly not an address. Learning takes place as people wrestle with the scripture text and discuss the questions. It is then that points raised in the chapters can be shared and discussed by group members. The leader's task is to provide a structure in which everyone feels it safe to participate. He or she should encourage everyone to take part appropriately, steer away from 'red herrings' and keep the group on the subject to hand.

Confidentiality: **Sometimes in small groups people are able to share matters of deep personal concern. Such matters should always be regarded as confidential, and must never become the subject of gossip.**

NOTES

Chapter 1: The Lord's Prayer in context

1 Michael Ramsey, *Be Still and Know*, Fount, 1982, p. 12.
2 Ramsey, *Be Still and Know*, p. 74.
3 Harry Williams, *Some Day I'll Find You*, Mitchell Beazley, 1982.
4 From 'De Oratione', quoted by C.F. Evans, *The Lord's Prayer*, SPCK, 1963, p. 1.
5 Brian Beck, *Christian Character in the Gospel of Luke*, Epworth Press, 1989, p. 69.
6 Frances Hogan, *Words of Life from Luke*, Fount, 1990, p. 148.
7 Oscar Cullman, *Prayer in the New Testament*, SCM Press, 1995, p. 40.
8 Brian J. Dodd, *Praying Jesus' Way*, IVP USA, 1997, p. 40.

Chapter 2: 'The end of all our exploring'

1 Anthony Bloom, *Living Prayer*, DLT, 1966.
2 H.A. Williams, *The True Wilderness*, Pelican, 1968, p. 19.

Chapter 3: 'Our Father who art in heaven'

1 Quoted in George Appleton (ed.), *The Oxford Book of Prayer*, OUP, 1987, p. 3.
2 Joachim Jeremias, *The Prayers of Jesus*, trans. John Bowden, SCM Press, 1967.
3 James Barr, 'Abba isn't Daddy', *Journal of Theological Studies* 39, 1988, pp. 28–47.
4 G.B. Caird, *Saint Luke*, Penguin, 1963, p. 152.
5 William Willimon and Stanley Hauerwas, *Lord, Teach Us*, Abingon Press, 1996.

Chapter 4: 'Hallowed be Thy name'

1 Michael Sadgrove, *Coventry Cathedral*, A Pitkin Guide, 1999, p. 3.
2 William Barclay, *The Plain Man Looks at the Lord's Prayer*, Fontana, 1964, p. 60.

Chapter 5: 'Thy kingdom come, Thy will be done on earth as it is in heaven'

1 Jeremias, *The Prayers of Jesus*, pp. 98–99.
2 Kenneth Slack, *Praying the Lord's Prayer Today*, SCM Press, 1973, p. 56.

3 Tom Wright, *The Lord and his Prayer*, SPCK Triangle, 1996, p. 27.
4 Wright, *The Lord and his Prayer*, p. 28.
5 A.M. Hunter, *The Parables, Then and Now*, SCM Press.
6 Wright, *The Lord and his Prayer*, p. 29.
7 Rob Warner, *Praying with Jesus*, Hodder, 1999, p. 52.

Chapter 6: 'Give us this day our daily bread'

1 Gerd Theissen, *The Open Door*, 1991, pp. 62–66.
2 Leonard Sweet, *Soul Tsunami*, Zondervan, 1999, p. 154.
3 Evans, *The Lord's Prayer*.
4 Ramsey, *Be Still and Know*, p. 30.
5 Wright, *The Lord and his Prayer*, pp. 39–40.
6 Ramsey, *Be Still and Know*, p. 74.

Chapter 7: 'Forgive us our trespasses as we forgive them that trespass against us'

1 Wright, *The Lord and his Prayer*, p. 50.
2 Leonard Griffith, *Hang on to the Lord's Prayer*, Upper Room, 1973.
3 Wright, *The Lord and his Prayer*, p. 55.
4 Philip Yancey, *What's So Amazing About Grace?* HarperCollins, 1997, p. 99.
5 J. Neville Ward, *Beyond Tomorrow*, Epworth Press, 1981, p. 74.
6 Yancey, *What's So Amazing About Grace?* p. 116.

Chapter 8: 'Lead us not into temptation, but deliver us from evil'

1 Slack, *Praying the Lord's Prayer Today*, p. 112.

Chapter 9: 'For thine is the kingdom, the power and the glory for ever and ever, Amen'

1 Quoted in Philip Yancey, *The Jesus I Never Knew*, Zondervan, 1995, p. 122.

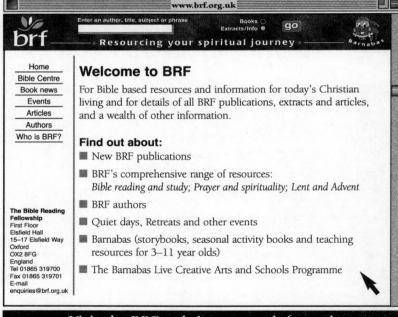

www.brf.org.uk

Enter an author, title, subject or phrase

Books ○
Extracts/Info ●

go

brf

Resourcing your spiritual journey

Barnabas

Home
Bible Centre
Book news
Events
Articles
Authors
Who is BRF?

**The Bible Reading
Fellowship**
First Floor
Elsfield Hall
15–17 Elsfield Way
Oxford
OX2 8FG
England
Tel 01865 319700
Fax 01865 319701
E-mail
enquiries@brf.org.uk

Welcome to BRF

For Bible based resources and information for today's Christian living and for details of all BRF publications, extracts and articles, and a wealth of other information.

Find out about:

■ New BRF publications

■ BRF's comprehensive range of resources:
Bible reading and study; Prayer and spirituality; Lent and Advent

■ BRF authors

■ Quiet days, Retreats and other events

■ Barnabas (storybooks, seasonal activity books and teaching resources for 3–11 year olds)

■ The Barnabas Live Creative Arts and Schools Programme

Visit the BRF website at www.brf.org.uk

BRF is a Registered Charity